A Reconnaissance of Selected Organic Compounds in Streams in Tribal Lands in Central Oklahoma, January–February 2009

By Carol J. Becker

Prepared in cooperation with the U.S. Environmental Protection Agency and the Kickapoo Tribe of Oklahoma

Scientific Investigations Report 2010–5110
Revised August 2010

U.S. Department of the Interior
U.S. Geological Survey

U.S. Department of the Interior
KEN SALAZAR, Secretary

U.S. Geological Survey
Marcia K. McNutt, Director

U.S. Geological Survey, Reston, Virginia: 2010

This and other USGS information products are available at http://store.usgs.gov/
U.S. Geological Survey
Box 25286, Denver Federal Center
Denver, CO 80225

To learn about the USGS and its information products visit http://www.usgs.gov/
1-888-ASK-USGS

Suggested citation:
Becker, C.J., 2010, A Reconnaissance of selected organic compounds in streams in tribal lands in Central Oklahoma, January–February 2009: U.S. Geological Survey Scientific Investigations Report 2010–5110, 46 p. (Revised August 2010)

Contents

Figures

Tables

Conversion Factors

Multiply	By	To obtain
Length		
inch (in)	2.54	centimeter (cm)
mile (mi)	1.61	kilometer (km)
Area		
square mile (mi^2)	2.59	square kilometer (km^2)
Flow rate		
cubic foot per second (ft^3/s)	0.028	cubic meter per second (m^3/s)

Laboratory reporting level (LRL)—LRLs are the smallest measured compound concentration that the laboratory could accurately measure for the analytical method used. LRLs were calculated using the lowest equipment calibration standards with the assumption that the compound spike had a 100 percent recovery and that there were no interferences from the sample matrix (Duane Wydoski, U.S. Geological Survey, National Water Quality Laboratory, written commun., 2009). The value of the LRL was reported with a "less than" remark code for samples in which the analyte was not detected.

Horizontal coordinate information is referenced to the North American Datum of 1983 (NAD 83).

Concentrations of chemical constituents in water are estimated and given in nanogram of compound per liter of water (ng/L). Compound concentrations measured in extracts are reported in nanogram per ampoule of extract from a composite of three SPMD or three POCIS media in each sampler.

A Reconnaissance of Selected Organic Compounds in Streams in Tribal Lands in Central Oklahoma, January– February 2009

By Carol J. Becker

Abstract

The U.S. Geological Survey worked in cooperation with the U.S. Environmental Protection Agency and the Kickapoo Tribe of Oklahoma on two separate reconnaissance projects carried out concurrently. Both projects entailed the use of passive samplers as a sampling methodology to investigate the detection of selected organic compounds at stream sites in jurisdictional areas of several tribes in central Oklahoma during January–February 2009.

The focus of the project with the U.S. Environmental Protection Agency was the detection of pesticides and pesticide metabolites using Semipermeable Membrane Devices at five stream sites in jurisdictional areas of several tribes. The project with the Kickapoo Tribe of Oklahoma focused on the detection of pesticides, pesticide metabolites, polycyclic aromatic hydrocarbons, polychlorinated biphenyl compounds, and synthetic organic compounds using Semipermeable Membrane Devices and Polar Organic Chemical Integrative Samplers at two stream sites adjacent to the Kickapoo tribal lands. The seven stream sites were located in central Oklahoma on the Cimarron River, Little River, North Canadian River, Deep Fork, and Washita River.

Extracts from SPMDs submerged at five stream sites, in cooperation with the U.S. Environmental Protection Agency, were analyzed for 46 pesticides and 6 pesticide metabolites. Dacthal, a pre-emergent herbicide, was detected at all five sites. Pendimethalin, also a pre-emergent, was detected at one site. The insecticides chlorpyrifos and dieldrin were detected at three sites and p,p'-DDE, a metabolite of the insecticide DDT, also was detected at three sites.

SPMDs and POCIS were submerged at the upstream edge and downstream edge of the Kickapoo tribal boundaries. Both sites are downstream from the Oklahoma City metropolitan area and multiple municipal wastewater treatment plants. Extracts from the passive samplers were analyzed for 62 pesticides, 10 pesticide metabolites, 3 polychlorinated biphenyl compounds, 35 polycyclic aromatic hydrocarbons, and 49 synthetic organic compounds.

Ten pesticides and four pesticide metabolites were detected at the upstream site and seven pesticides and four pesticide metabolites were detected at the downstream site. Pesticides detected at both sites were atrazine, chlorpyrifos, dacthal, dieldrin, metolachlor, pendimethalin, and trans-nonachlor. Additionally at the upstream site, heptachlor, pentachlorophenol, and prometon were detected. The pesticide metabolites p,p'-DDE, cis-chlordane, and trans-chlordane also were detected at both sites.

Polychlorinated biphenyl compounds aroclor-1016/1242, aroclor-1254, and aroclor-1260 were detected at both sites. The upstream site had 16 polycyclic aromatic hydrocarbon detections and the downstream site had 8 detections. Because of chromatographic interference during analysis, a positive identification of 17 polycyclic aromatic hydrocarbons could not be made. Consequently, there may have been a greater number of these compounds detected at both sites.

A total of 36 synthetic organic compounds were detected at the two sites adjacent to the Kickapoo tribal lands. The upstream site had 21 synthetic organic compound detections: three detergent metabolites, two fecal indicators, three flame retardants, seven industrial compounds, five compounds related to personal care products, and beta-sitosterol, a plant sterol. Fifteen synthetic organic compounds were detected at the downstream site and included: one fecal indicator, three flame retardants, six industrial compounds, and five compounds related to personal care products.

Introduction

Sovereign tribal lands encompass a large part of central Oklahoma (fig. 1). The gathering of aquatic plants and animals and particularly fish for consumption from streams is a common cultural practice with tribal members. Pesticides and other types of synthetic organic compounds (SOCs) are a concern to tribal members and the people who use streams as a source of food and recreation.

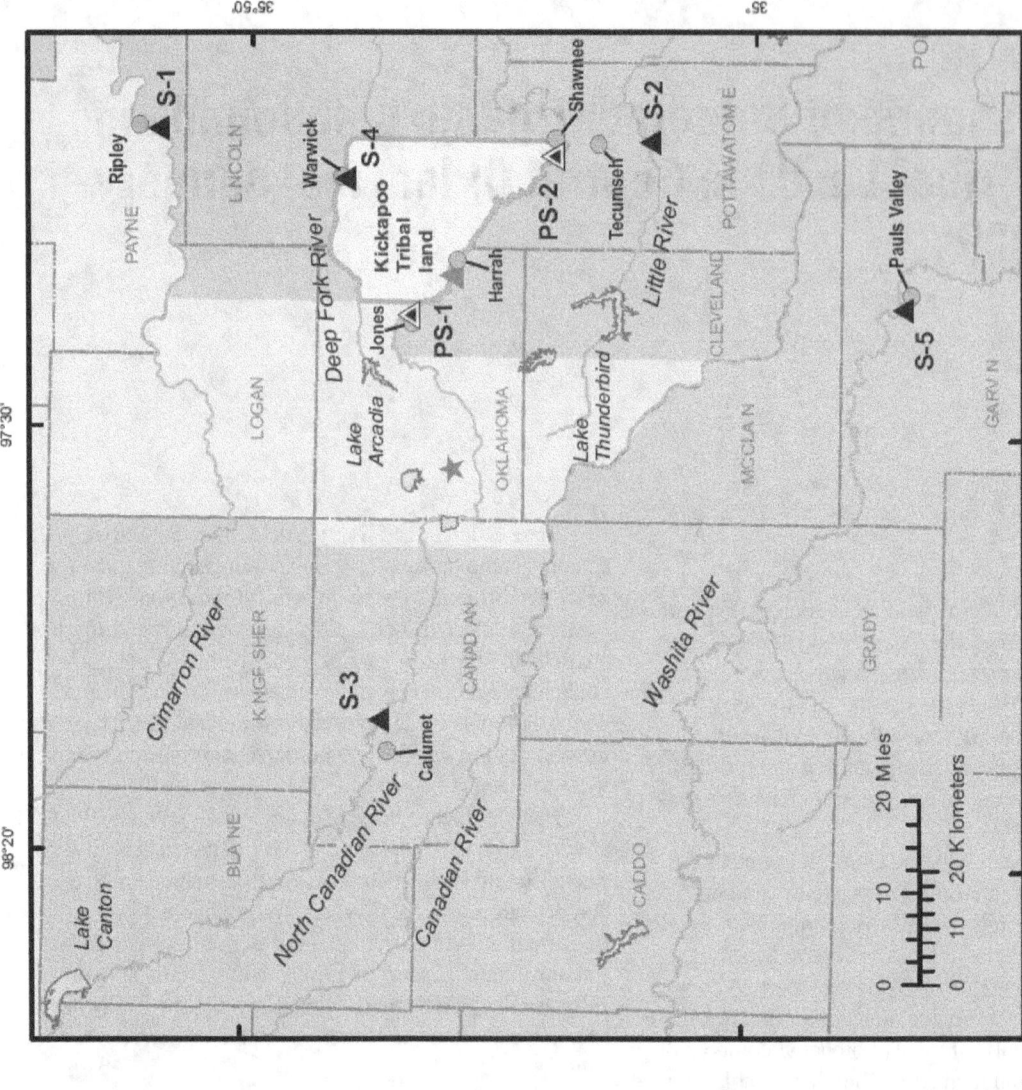

EXPLANATION

Tribal lands

Town

Oklahoma City

U.S. Stream-gaging station on North Canadian River near Harrah Oklahoma (07241550) and site identifier

U.S. Geological Survey stream-gaging station (identification number) where Semipermeable Membrane Devices were deployed (in cooperation with the U.S. Environmental Protection Agency)

S-1   Cimarron River near Ripley Oklahoma (07161450) and site identifier

S-2   Little River near Tecumseh Oklahoma (07230500) and site identifier

S-3   North Canadian River near Calumet Oklahoma (07239450) and site identifier

S-4   Deep Fork at Warwick Oklahoma (07242380) and site identifier

S-5   Washita River near Pauls Valley Oklahoma (07328500) and site identifier

Stream site (identification number) where Semipermeable Membrane Devices and Polar Organic Integrative Samplers were deployed (in cooperation with the Kickapoo Tribe of Oklahoma)

PS-1   North Canadian River at Hogback Road near Jones Oklahoma (07241540) and site identifier

PS-2   North Canadian River near Shawnee Oklahoma (07241700) and site identifier

Figure 1.   Location of U.S. Geological Survey stream-gaging stations and stream sites where passive samplers where submerged in jurisdictional areas of several tribes in central Oklahoma, January–February 2009.

A wide variety of SOCs are used today in agriculture, pharmaceuticals, chemical manufacturing, and personal care products. These compounds may enter streams in surface-water runoff from agricultural and urban land-use areas and in treated wastewater effluent from municipal wastewater treatment plants. The detection and types of SOCs in groundwater and surface water have been the focus of many studies over the last decade (Galloway and others, 2004; Masoner and Mashburn, 2004; Tertuliani and others, 2008). The frequency with which these compounds are detected in streams was shown by Kolpin and others (2002) in a study that found 80 percent of 139 streams sampled across the United States had detectable concentrations. Many of these compounds are suspected or are known endocrine disruptors that can influence or interfere with the hormonal system of growing organisms (Rhomberg and Seeley, 2005; Tulane and Xavier Universities, 2009a) causing reproductive and developmental problems. In humans, the potential health effects are debatable, but research has shown that the consumption of low concentrations of SOCs or mixtures can contribute to female reproductive disorders (Crain and others, 2008). There also is speculation of other health concerns, especially to growing embryos and fetuses (Tulane and Xavier Universities, 2009b).

In an effort to look more closely at pesticides and other types of SOCs in streams in Oklahoma, the U.S. Geological Survey (USGS) Oklahoma Water Science Center worked in cooperation with the U.S. Environmental Protection Agency (US EPA) and the Kickapoo Tribe of Oklahoma on two separate but similar reconnaissance projects carried out concurrently. Both projects entailed the use of passive samplers, Semipermeable Membrane Devices (SPMD) and Polar Organic Chemical Integrative Sampler (POCIS) as a surface-water sampling methodology to detect SOCs.

Purpose and Scope

The purpose of this report is to describe the results from a reconnaissance of selected organic compounds in streams, performed from January 15 through February 19, 2009 that used passive samplers at seven stream sites in jurisdictional areas of several tribes (fig. 1 and table 1).

In cooperation with the Kickapoo Tribe of Oklahoma, SPMDs and POCIS were submerged at two stream sites, referred to as PS-1 and PS-2, on the North Canadian River in Oklahoma and Pottawatomie counties adjacent to the

Table 1. U.S. Geological Survey stream-gaging stations, stream sites, and sample information for passive samplers submerged in jurisdictional areas of several tribes in central Oklahoma, January–February 2009.

[USGS, U.S. Geological Survey; POCIS, Polar Organic Chemical Integrative Sampler; SPMD, Semipermeable Membrane Device; PAH, polycyclic aromatic hydrocarbon; PCB, polychlorinated biphenyl compound; SOC, synthetic organic compound]

USGS station number	Site identifier	USGS stream-gaging station	Passive sampler type deployed	Types and number of organic compounds analyzed	Laboratory method
USGS stream-gaging stations where passive samplers were submerged in cooperation with the U.S. Environmental Protection Agency					
07161450	S-1	Cimarron River near Ripley, Oklahoma	SPMD	46 Pesticides, 6 metabolites	Zaugg and others (1995)
07230500	S-2	Little River near Tecumseh, Oklahoma	SPMD	46 Pesticides, 6 metabolites	Zaugg and others (1995)
07239450	S-3	North Canadian River near Calumet, Oklahoma	SPMD	46 Pesticides, 6 metabolites	Zaugg and others (1995)
07242380	S-4	Deep Fork at Warwick, Oklahoma	SPMD	46 Pesticides, 6 metabolites	Zaugg and others (1995)
07328500	S-5	Washita River near Pauls Valley, Oklahoma	SPMD	46 Pesticides, 6 metabolites	Zaugg and others (1995)
Stream sites where passive samplers were submerged in cooperation with the Kickapoo Tribe of Oklahoma					
07241540	PS-1	North Canadian River at Hogback Road near Jones, Oklahoma	POCIS SPMD	62 pesticides, 10 metabolites, 3 PCBs, 35 PAHs, 49 SOCs	Noriega and others (2004); Zaugg and others (1995; 2006; 2007)
07241700	PS-2	North Canadian River near Shawnee, Oklahoma	POCIS SPMD	62 pesticides, 10 metabolites, 3 PCBs, 35 PAHs, 49 SOCs	Noriega and others (2004); Zaugg and others (1995; 2006; 2007)

Kickapoo tribal lands (fig. 1). Sites PS-1 and PS-2 were about 9 miles upstream and about 24 miles downstream, respectively, from the USGS stream-gaging station North Canadian River near Harrah, Oklahoma (fig. 1 and table 1). Extracts from the POCIS and SPMDs deployed at PS-1 and PS-2, were analyzed for 62 pesticides, 10 pesticide metabolites, 3 polychlorinated biphenyl compounds (PCB), 35 polycyclic aromatic hydrocarbons (PAH), and 49 SOCs by using the laboratory methodologies described by Noriega and others (2004) and Zaugg and others (1995; 2006; 2007). Nine pesticides, one metabolite, and eight PAHs were analyzed by using more than one laboratory methodology.

In cooperation with the US EPA, SPMDs were submerged at five stream sites, referred to as S-1 through S-5, located at USGS stream-gaging stations; Cimarron River near Ripley, Oklahoma (07161450), Little River near Tecumseh, Oklahoma (07230500), North Canadian River near Calumet, Oklahoma (07239450), Deep Fork at Warwick, Oklahoma (07242380), and the Washita River near Pauls Valley, Oklahoma (07328500) in Payne, Pottawatomie, Canadian, Lincoln, and Garvin counties (respectively) in central Oklahoma (fig. 1 and table 1). Extracts from the SPMDs were analyzed for 46 pesticides and 6 pesticide metabolites by using the laboratory methodology described in Zaugg and others (1995) (appendixes 1 and 2). Approximate concentrations in water were calculated for the pesticides and pesticide metabolites and are shown in appendix 3.

Land Use/Cover and Streamflow Conditions

Land use/cover has an effect on the types and frequencies of pesticides detected in surface water. USGS studies between 1992 and 2001 showed that pesticides were most frequently detected in agricultural and urban areas and the types detected were primarily those with the greatest use (Gilliom and others, 2006). Streams in urban areas had higher detections of insecticides and herbicides used for nonagricultural purposes. Pesticides that were most frequently detected in agricultural and urban areas were atrazine, metolachlor, prometon, and simazine, and the atrazine metabolite deethylatrazine.

Land use/cover varies in Oklahoma from grassland and agriculture in the west to hay/pasture and forest in the east (fig. 2). The greatest density of urban development in the study area is in Oklahoma County in and surrounding Oklahoma City.

In agricultural areas, cultivated crops are dominated by the production of wheat, with alfalfa, sorghum, and other small grain crops grown in smaller amounts. Pesticides are generally applied during the growing season from spring to autumn to control weeds, insects, and fungus on crops. Correspondingly, pesticides are a much greater concern in streams and groundwater during these times of the year. Pesticide use during winter is negligible in Oklahoma, but pre-emergent herbicides are used occasionally to deter the growth of winter grasses for the wheat spring growing season (Brad Tipton, Canadian County

Agriculture Educator, written commun., 2008). Herbicides commonly applied for weed control during the winter months in Canadian County are sulfonylurea compounds which were not analyzed in this study.

Grassland covers the largest percentage of land in the upstream basins for five of the six gages, including the Harrah gage near sites PS-1 and PS-2 (table 2). Upstream from the Tecumseh gage, deciduous forest covers the largest percentage of land and grassland the second. Cultivated crops are the second largest land use in the upstream basins of the Ripley, Calumet, Harrah, and Pauls Valley gages. Urban development is the third largest land use upstream from the Tecumseh, Harrah, and Warwick gages making up 11, 4, and 16, percent, respectively.

The Ripley gage at S-1 has the largest upstream drainage area of 17,979 square miles (mi^2) and the largest annual mean streamflow of 2,236 cubic feet per second (ft^3/s) during the period of record 1988 to 2008 (table 2). The Tecumseh gage at S-2 has the smallest upstream drainage area of 456 mi^2 and the smallest annual mean streamflow of 146 ft^3/s (period of record 1965 to 2009). Streamflow data are available from the USGS National Water Information System website, *http://waterdata.usgs.gov/nwis*.

The Calumet gage, at S-3 has an upstream drainage area of 12,962 mi^2 and an annual mean streamflow of 268 ft^3/s during the period of record 1988 to 2008 (table 2). An increase in streamflow, not related to precipitation, is periodically measured at the Calumet gage as a result of releases from Lake Canton about 60 miles upstream. The effect on streamflow from a release can be seen on figure 3 beginning on February 15, as an increase from 80 ft^3/s to 250 ft^3/s about 4 days before the passive sampler was retrieved.

The Warwick gage at S-4, has the second smallest drainage area of 532 mi^2 and the second smallest annual mean streamflow of 260 ft^3/s, during the period of record 1988 to 2008 (table 2). The headwaters of the basin upstream from the Warwick gage begin in the northern parts of the Oklahoma City metropolitan area and flow into Lake Arcadia, which is the primary source of streamflow to the Deep Fork (fig. 1). Streamflow periodically increases because of releases from Lake Arcadia. The effects on streamflow are shown on figure 3, as an increase of about 60 ft^3/s beginning on February 23, 2009 about 4 days after the passive sampler was retrieved.

The Harrah station, near sites PS-1 and PS-2, has an upstream drainage area of 13,501 mi^2 and an annual mean streamflow of 500 ft^3/s during the period of record 1969 to 2008 (table 2). Streamflow on the North Canadian River near the Harrah gage is periodically affected by water released from upstream reservoirs and from a series of low-water weirs adjacent to Oklahoma City. Streamflow also may be affected by periodic releases of treated effluent from multiple upstream municipal wastewater treatment plants, but the magnitude of these effects is unknown. Releases from upstream reservoirs are apparent on figure 3 as an increase in streamflow beginning on February 19.

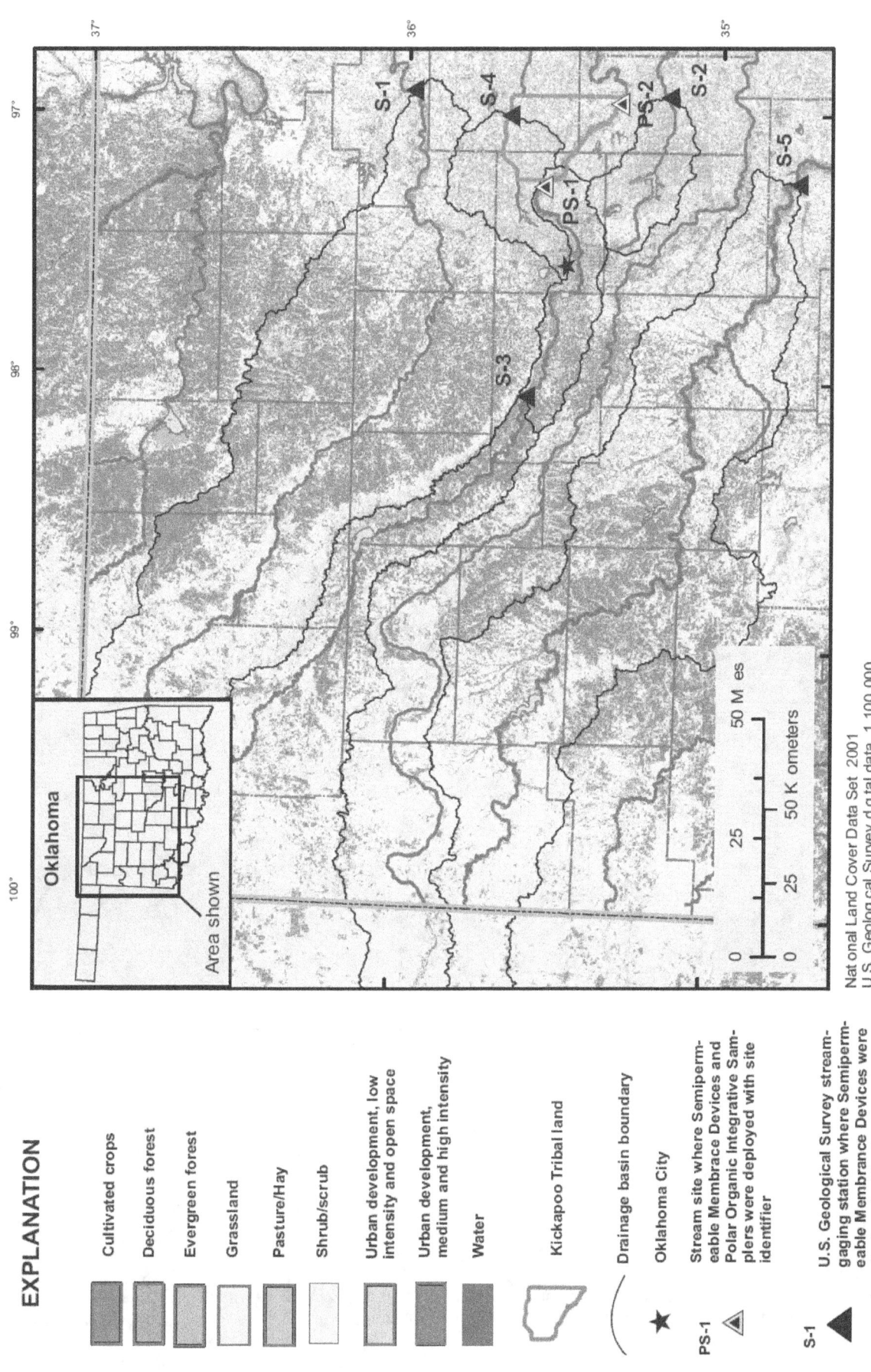

EXPLANATION

Cultivated crops

Deciduous forest

Evergreen forest

Grassland

Pasture/Hay

Shrub/scrub

Urban development, low intensity and open space

Urban development, medium and high intensity

Water

Kickapoo Tribal land

Drainage basin boundary

Oklahoma City

PS-1   Stream site where Semipermeable Membrance Devices and Polar Organic Integrative Samplers were deployed with site identifier

S-1   U.S. Geological Survey streamgaging station where Semipermeable Membrance Devices were deployed with site identifier

National Land Cover Data Set 2001
U S Geological Survey d g tal data 1 100 000
Albers Equal Area Con c project on North Amer can Datum 1983

50 M es

0   25   50 K ometers

Oklahoma

Area shown

Figure 2.   Land use/cover in central and western Oklahoma during 2001.

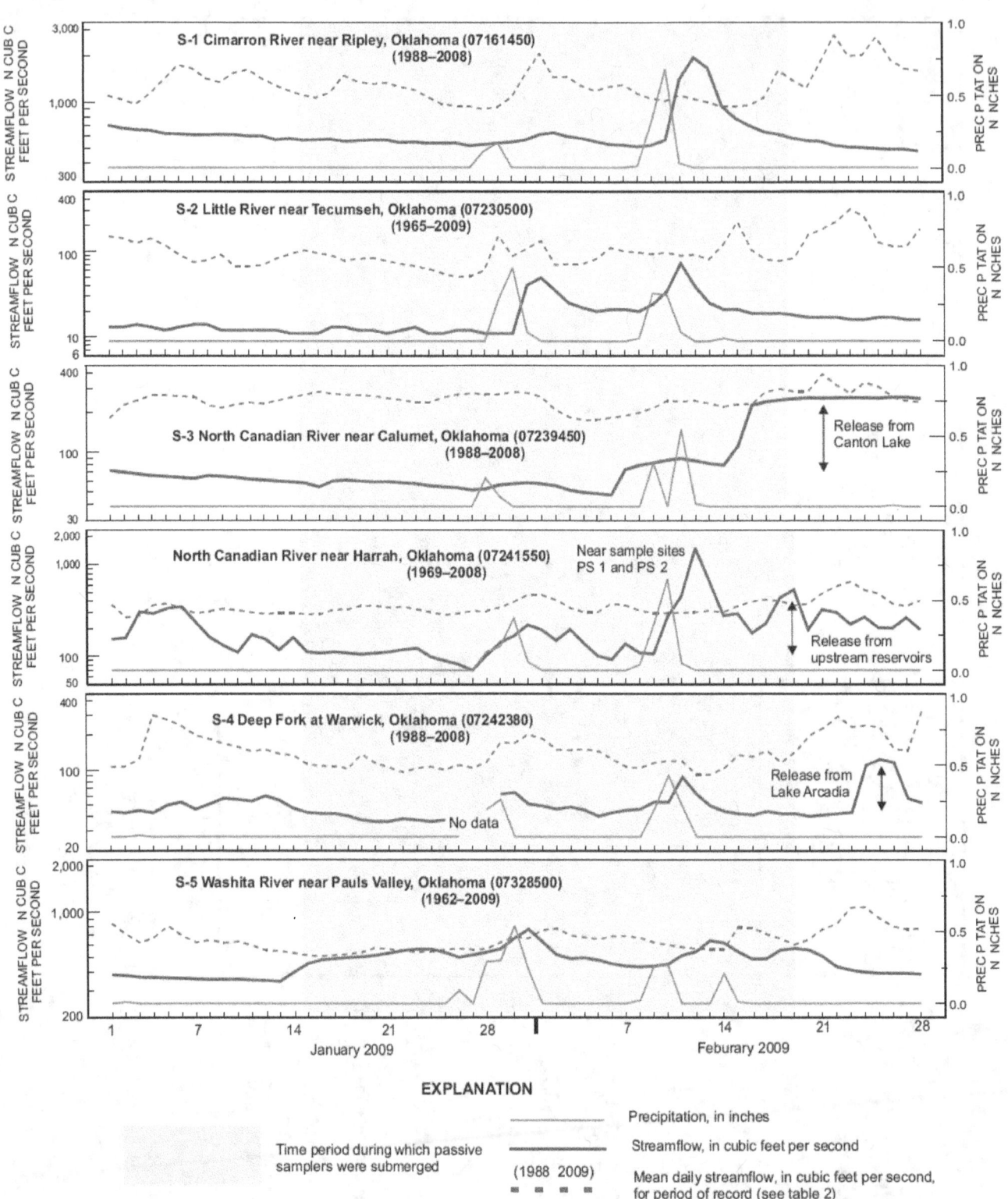

Figure 3. Hydrographs showing streamflow and precipitation during submergence of passive samplers and historical mean daily streamflows at U.S. geological Survey streamflow-gaging stations in jurisdictional areas of several tribes in central Oklahoma, January–February 2009.

Table 2. Historical streamflow statistics and upstream land use/cover for U.S. Geological Survey stream-gaging stations where passive samplers were submerged in jurisdictional areas of several tribes in central Oklahoma, January–February 2009.

[USGS, U.S. Geological Survey; ft³/s, cubic feet per second; mi², square miles]

USGS station number	Site identifier	U.S. Geological Survey stream-gaging station	Historical mean daily low flow/high flow for January 1 to February 28 (ft³/s)	Annual mean streamflow (ft³/s)	Period of record (water year)	Upstream drainage area / contributing drainage area (mi²)	Percentages of the three largest land use/cover categories in the upstream drainage basin
07161450	S-1	Cimarron River near Ripley, Oklahoma	902/ 2,730	2,236	1988/ 2008	17,979 / 13,053	48 percent grassland 35 percent cultivated crops 5 percent shrub/scrub
07230500	S-2	Little River near Tecumseh, Oklahoma	38/ 306	146	1965/ 2009	456 / 456	44 percent deciduous forest 35 percent grassland 11 percent urban development
07239450	S-3	North Canadian River near Calumet, Oklahoma	133/ 389	268	1988/ 2008	12,962 / 8,063	65 percent grassland 24 percent cultivated crops 6 percent shrub/scrub
07241550	near PS-1 and PS-2	North Canadian River near Harrah, Oklahoma	267/ 651	500	1969/ 2008	13,501 / 8,602	63 percent grassland 25 percent cultivated crops 4 percent urban development
07242380	S-4	Deep Fork at Warwick, Oklahoma	92/ 326	260	1988/ 2008	532 / 532	39 percent grassland 37 percent deciduous forest 16 percent urban development
07328500	S-5	Washita River near Pauls Valley, Oklahoma	509/ 1,070	965	1962/ 2009	5,330 / 5,330	50 percent grassland 28 percent cultivated crops 11 percent shrub/scrub

Acknowledgments

The author would like to thank Genevieve McGeisey and Darren Shields with the Kickapoo Tribe of Oklahoma for their assistance with the project. Appreciation also is given to Chad Ashworth, Mark Becker, Rick Hanlon, Stan Paxton, Ernie Smith, and Kim Winton at the USGS Oklahoma Water Science Center for their assistance with the project. The advice and guidance provided by Duane Wydoski at the USGS National Water Quality Laboratory in Denver, Colorado was invaluable. Thanks are given to Jason Masoner with the USGS Oklahoma Water Science Center and David Alvarez with the USGS Columbia Environmental Research Center for their peer reviews of the manuscript.

Methods of Study

SPMDs were deployed at all seven stream sites S-1 through S-5 and PS-1 and PS-2. POCIS were deployed, in addition to SPMDs, at stream sites PS-1 and PS-2. Both types of passive samplers were submerged in streams from January 15 through February 19 during low flow, when streamflow conditions generally were less than the daily mean flow for the period of record.

The SPMD and POCIS passive samplers have several advantages over surface-water grab samples. Passive samplers provide water-quality information during an integrated period of time, usually weeks, and during a range of hydrologic conditions. In contrast, grab samples are collected at a single point and only provide site-specific water-quality information for a snapshot in time. The extended exposure time of the passive samplers to water increases the likelihood of detecting constituents that might be in the stream only intermittently (Alvarez and others, 2004). Additionally, the SPMD media sequester chemicals similarly to aquatic biota and can provide information about the bioavailability of hydrophobic chemicals in streams not typically measured in water samples (Environmental Sampling Technologies, 2008).

Site Selection

Stream sites S-1 through S-5 were at USGS stream-gaging stations; whereas, PS-1 and PS-2 were near bridges about 9 miles upstream and about 24 miles downstream (respectively) from the stream-gaging station North Canadian River near Harrah, Oklahoma, (07241550) (fig. 1 and table 2). Sample sites PS-1 and PS-2 were selected on the upstream and downstream boundaries of the Kickapoo tribal land. Multiple upstream wastewater treatment plants (2009) are permitted to discharge treated wastewater effluent into the North Canadian River (Oklahoma Department of Environmental Quality, 2009) upstream from the Kickapoo tribal boundary (fig. 1). The PS-1 sample site was at the western edge of the tribal boundary upstream from areas used by the tribe for ceremonies. Sample-site PS-2 was established downstream on the eastern edge of the tribal boundary to detect pesticides and other types of SOCs leaving the tribal jurisdictional area.

Deployment sites were selected where stream depth and flow were adequate for the entire period of submergence. The sampler had to remain submerged in moving water and placed so it could be safely deployed and retrieved during high flow, if necessary. The sampler also needed to be where the chance of floating debris and vandalism were minimal.

Passive Samplers

Three SPMDs in a canister were deployed at each stream site. Each SPMD consisted of lipid-filled polyethylene tubing, 91.4 centimeters long and 2.5 centimeters wide, wound around posts on a support rack to maximize surface exposure. The polyethylene tubing has transport properties that selectively allow hydrophobic compounds in water to partition into the SPMD and be retained by the membrane and a thin film of triolein (lipid). The lipid and membrane collectively sequesters the compounds that are later extracted and analyzed (Environmental Sampling Technologies, 2008).

The triolein was spiked before deployment with four polychlorinated biphenyl compounds (PCB-4, 14, 29, and 50) that were used as performance reference compounds (PRC). As described in detail by Huckins and others (2006) and Tertuliani and others (2008) the PRCs provide an estimate of SPMD sampling rates at each sample site, which varies depending on environmental factors such as temperature, water velocity, and membrane biofouling. The rate of PRC loss from the SPMD membranes during stream submergence was compared to that of the PRC loss during laboratory calibration studies to derive an exposure adjustment factor, which was used to determine more accurate in situ sampling rates. This information was used in combination with SOC partition coefficients and concentrations measured in sample extracts to estimate time-weighted water concentrations by using the exposure models created by Huckins and others (2006) and the U.S. Geological Survey, Columbia Environmental Research Center (2006).

Three POCIS in a canister were deployed only at stream sites PS-1 and PS-2. Each POCIS is composed of sorbent materials enveloped by a microporous polyethersulfone membrane. The membrane allows dissolved constituents to flow through and be sequestered while filtering out sediment and debris (U.S. Geological Survey, Columbia Environmental Research Center, 2004). The POCIS was used to sample for dissolved SOCs that included selected pesticides, detergent metabolites, fecal indicators, flame retardants, industrial compounds, and compounds related to personal care products

(appendix 1). The compounds were later extracted from the sorbent and analyzed.

Deployment and Retrieval of Passive Samplers

The SPMDs and POCIS were purchased from Environmental Sampling Technologies, St. Joseph, Missouri, and were sent to the USGS Oklahoma Water Science Center surrounded by argon gas in sealed metal cans. The cans containing the SPMDs were kept at -20° Celsius until the day of deployment and then chilled on ice until submergence at the deployment sites.

During deployment the SPMDs and POCIS media, preloaded on support racks, were removed from the original metal cans and placed in a protective stainless steel canister as quickly as possible. The support racks were handled with clean gloved hands and SPMD and POCIS surfaces were not touched or abraded. USGS personnel refrained from the use of personal care products and caffeine on the day of deployment.

Canisters at six stream sites were secured to T-posts with a length of stainless steel chain and one canister was secured to the bridge. During retrieval, canisters were moved from the water and the passive samplers on the support racks were removed and returned to the original metal cans, sealed, and placed on ice. The sealed cans were transported back to USGS Oklahoma Water Science Center and were stored at -20° Celsius until being placed on ice and shipped overnight to Environmental Sampling Technologies for extraction.

Extraction Procedure

The sequestered SOCs were extracted from the SPMDs and POCIS by Environmental Sampling Technologies. SOCs in the POCIS were extracted with 40 milliliters of methanol and concentrated under ultra high purity nitrogen. The extracts were transferred to methanol, filtered through a glass fiber filter (Fisher, G-6) and quantitatively transferred to 2-milliliter amber ampoules (Terri Spencer, Environmental Sampling Technologies, written commun., 2009).

Briefly, SOCs and performance reference compounds were extracted from the SPMDs by dialysis in hexane, concentrated by using the Kuderna-Danish method (Dean, 2010), reduced in volume under ultra high purity nitrogen to about 0.5 milliliter, and then filtered through a glass fiber filter (Fisher, G-6) by using methylene chloride. Sample volumes were again reduced under ultra high purity nitrogen and quantitatively transferred to auto sampler vials by using methylene chloride as the transfer solvent. Samples underwent final clean-up by gel permeation chromatography, were again reduced in volume with ultra high purity nitrogen, and quantitatively transferred with methylene chloride to 2-milliliter amber ampoules (Terri Spencer, Environmental Sampling Technologies, written commun., 2009).

The final SPMD and POCIS extracts for each sampling site were a composite of the three samplers in a canister for each sampler type. Similarly, the field blanks were combined into an extract for each sampler type.

Laboratory Analysis

SPMD and POCIS extracts were analyzed by the USGS National Water Quality Laboratory (NWQL) in Lakewood, Colorado using custom methodologies (Duane Wydoski, U.S. Geological Survey, National Water Quality Laboratory, written commun., 2009). SPMD extracts from the sites S-1 through S-5 and PS-1 and PS-2 were analyzed for 46 pesticides and 6 pesticide metabolites by using the technique described in Zaugg and others (1995). The methylene chloride solvent containing the extracts was replaced by a mixture of ethyl acetate and toluene. The solvent mixture was then analyzed by using gas chromatography/mass spectrometry by positive ion electron-impact ionization in the selected-ion mode. Each compound was identified in the extract by comparing curves to analytical standards and National Institute of Science and Technology reference spectra. The compound concentration in the extract was determined by using a six-point curve based on calibration that was normalized to internal standards.

A portion of the PS-1 and PS-2 SPMD extracts was replaced with hexane and analyzed for 14 pesticides, 4 pesticide metabolites and 3 PCB compounds by using the technique described in Noriega and others (2004) (appendix 4). The extracts were cleaned by using alumina/silica combined column adsorption chromatography and were split into two fractions. The second fraction underwent an additional adsorption chromatography step by using a Florisil column for cleanup. Both fractions were analyzed by dual capillary-column gas chromatography with electron-capture detection that was calibrated for both capillary columns by using multipoint calibration standards. The compound concentrations in the extracts were determined by using a six-point curve based on calibration standards that were normalized to internal standards.

SPMD extracts from PS-1 and PS-2 also were analyzed for 2 pesticides, 32 PAHs, and 4 SOCs (appendixes 1 and 4) and performance reference compounds by using the instrumental conditions described in Zaugg and others (2006). The extracts in methylene chloride were analyzed by using gas chromatography/mass spectrometry by positive ion electron-impact ionization in the selected-ion mode. Each compound was identified in the extract by comparing curves to analytical standards and National Institute of Science and Technology reference spectra. Compound concentration in the extract was determined by using a six-point curve based on calibration standards that were normalized to internal standards.

POCIS extracts from PS-1 and PS-2 were analyzed for 8 pesticides, 11 PAHs, and 43 SOCs, many of which are considered indicators of wastewater effluent (appendixes 1 and 4), by using the technique and instrumental conditions described in Zaugg and others (2007). The extracts in methylene chloride, in addition to a set of multiple-level analytical standard solutions, were analyzed by full scan positive-ion gas chromatography/mass spectrometry in the electron-impact mode.

Quality Control

Quality control blanks were used to assess unintentional contamination in the field and in the laboratory. A field blank consisting of three SPMDs was processed with the SPMDs deployed at sites S-1 through S-5. A second field blank consisting of three SPMDs and three POCIS was processed with samplers deployed at PS-1 and PS-2.

Laboratory blanks and spikes were used by NWQL to assess the preparation, analyte recovery, and to check the performance of the analytical methods. Field and laboratory blanks and spike information are shown on appendixes 2 and 4.

Data Reporting

The detection or nondetection of a compound is used for descriptive and comparative purposes in the report and not the laboratory or calculated water concentrations. A compound was considered detected if it was measured in the extract at a concentration three times, or greater, than the highest concentration measured in the field or laboratory blank.

Compound concentrations measured in extracts are reported in nanogram per ampoule of extract from a composite of three SPMD or three POCIS media in each sampler. These extract concentrations are shown in appendixes 2 and 4. Approximate water concentrations in nanogram per liter (ng/L) were calculated for selected pesticides, PCB compounds, and PAHs (appendixes 3 and 4).

Compound concentrations are reported above the laboratory reporting level which is the smallest measured compound concentration that the laboratory could accurately measure for the analytical method used. Laboratory reporting levels were calculated by using the lowest equipment calibration standards with the assumption that the compound spike had a 100 percent recovery with no interferences from the sample matrix (Duane Wydoski, U.S. Geological Survey, National Water Quality Laboratory, written commun., 2009).

The presence of many compounds could not be positively identified at less than the laboratory reporting level because of chromatographic interference during analysis at the laboratory. These concentrations are preceded by a less than sign (<) and are considered nondetections.

Seventeen compounds were analyzed in the SPMD and POCIS extracts from PS-1 and PS-2 by two different laboratory methodologies. Dieldrin and p, p'-DDE were the only compounds detected in both sampler extracts; both compounds are counted only once as a detection in the report.

Selected Organic Compounds in Streams in Tribal Lands

Extracts from the SPMDs deployed at S-1 through S-5 were analyzed for 46 pesticides and 6 pesticide metabolites (appendix 2). Extracts from the POCIS and SPMDs deployed at PS-1 and PS-2, were analyzed for, 10 pesticide metabolites, 3 PCBs, 35 PAHs, and 49 SOCs. Nine pesticides, one pesticide metabolite, and eight PAHs were analyzed in extracts from samplers deployed at the two sites by using more than one laboratory methodology. Approximate concentrations in water were calculated for selected pesticides and pesticide metabolites and are shown in appendixes 3 and 4.

Pesticides and Pesticide Metabolites

Sites S-1 through S-5 had one to four pesticides detected of the 46 analyzed in SPMD extracts (fig. 4). Sites PS-1 and PS-2 had 10 and seven pesticides detected, respectively, of the 62 pesticides analyzed in extracts from both sampler types (fig. 5 and appendix 4). All seven sites had detections of dacthal, a preemergent herbicide. Three sites, PS-1, PS-2, and S-4 also had detections of pendimethalin, a pre-emergent herbicide. Five sites (excluding S-2 and S-3) had detections of the insecticides dieldrin and chlorpyrifos. Chlorpyrifos, commonly called Dursban, was banned for domestic use in June 2000 but is still used for agriculture, wood treatment, and on golf courses (U.S. Environmental Protection Agency, 2002b). Five sites had detections of p,p'-DDE, a metabolite of the insecticide DDT. Dieldrin and DDT are organochlorine pesticides that were banned in the U.S. more than 20 years ago and are referred to as legacy pesticides because of persistence and widespread detection in the environment (Gilliom and others, 2006),

In addition to the four pesticides detected at S-1 through S-5, the herbicides atrazine, metolachlor, pentachlorophenol, and prometon and the insecticides heptachlor and trans-nonachlor were detected at PS-1; atrazine, metolachlor, and trans-nonachlor also were detected at PS-2. The pesticide metabolites, cis-chlordane and trans-chlordane, of the legacy insecticide chlordane, also were detected at sites PS-1 and PS-2. These pesticides and pesticide metabolites, except for dacthal, metolachlor, and prometon, are suspected or are known to have endocrine disruptor potential (Kegley and others, 2008).

Concentrations of three detected pesticides and one metabolite are regulated in public-drinking water by the US

EPA with maximum contaminant levels (MCLs) of atrazine (3,000 ng/L), heptachlor (400 ng/L), heptachlor epoxide (200 ng/L), and pentachlorophenol (1,000 ng/L) (U.S. Environmental Protection Agency, 2009a). All four compounds have potential health effects from ingestion ranging from reproduction problems to an increased risk of cancer (U.S. Environmental Protection Agency, 2009a). However, based on SPMD results, the approximate water concentrations of heptachlor and heptachlor epoxide representing stream samples are small, about 2,000 to 4,000 times smaller than the respective MCLs in drinking water. The water concentrations of atrazine and pentachlorophenol could not be estimated because these two compounds were sequestered by the POCIS sampler, which did not have PRCs needed for the calculations.

Increases in concentrations of many water-quality constituents were detected in the downstream direction of the North Canadian River from the Calumet station to the Harrah station by Brigham and others (2002). A summary of water-quality data from 1988 to 1999 showed that while specific conductance and concentrations of dissolved solids and sulfate decreased in the downstream direction, chloride, total dissolved concentrations of nitrogen and phosphorus compounds, and many pesticides increased in the downstream direction. Increases in chloride and nutrient concentrations may be related to effluent from wastewater treatment plants but also can result from urban runoff or natural sources. Brigham and others (2002) reported that the frequencies of detection for 12 of 13 pesticides increased between the Calumet gage and the Harrah gage. Pesticides having the highest frequencies of detection (in 44 to 63 samples) at the Harrah gage were the herbicides 2,4-D (83 percent), atrazine (17 percent), and simazine(67 percent), and the insecticides diazinon (90 percent), dieldrin (82 percent), and lindane (96 percent). The frequencies of detection ranged from 77 percent for atrazine and 96 percent for lindane.

Brigham and others (2002) reported that the herbicide 2,4-D and the insecticide lindane were the most frequently detected pesticides in stream samples collected at four sites on the North Canadian River from 1988 to 1999. Atrazine and dieldrin were detected at sites PS-1 and PS-2 (near the Harrah gage), whereas, diazinon, lindane, and simazine were not. 2,4-D was not analyzed in this study.

Nationwide, Gilliom and others (2006) reported that USGS studies from 1992 to 2001 showed that the pesticides most frequently detected in streams draining agricultural and urban areas were the herbicides atrazine, metolachlor, prometon, and simazine, and the metabolite of atrazine, deethylatrazine. None of these compounds were detected at sites S-1 through S-5. At sites PS-1 and PS-2, atrazine and metolachlor were detected in addition to prometon, a nonagricultural herbicide, at PS-1.

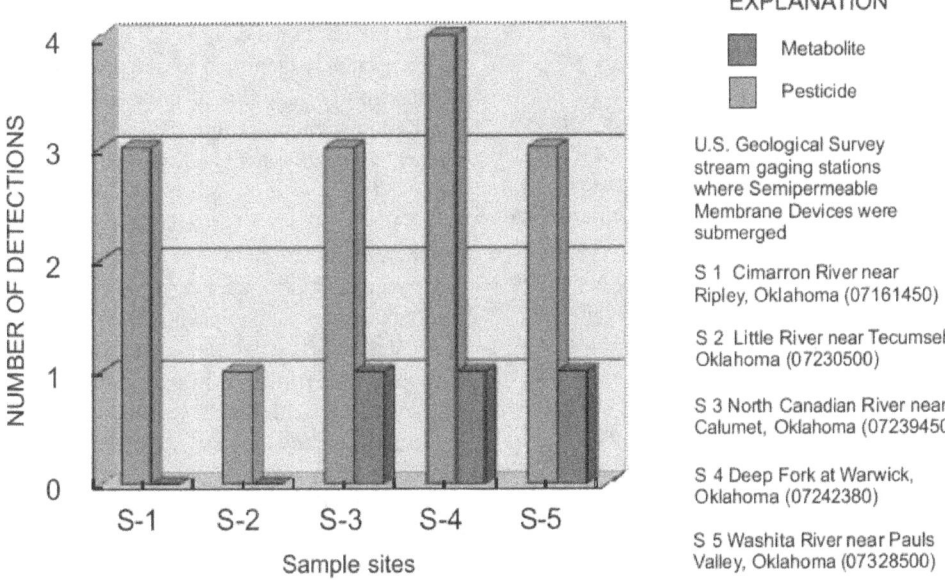

Figure 4. The number of pesticides and pesticide metabolites detected in extracts from Semipermeable Membrane Devices submerged at U.S. Geological Survey stream-gaging stations in jurisdictional areas of several tribes in central Oklahoma, January–February 2009.

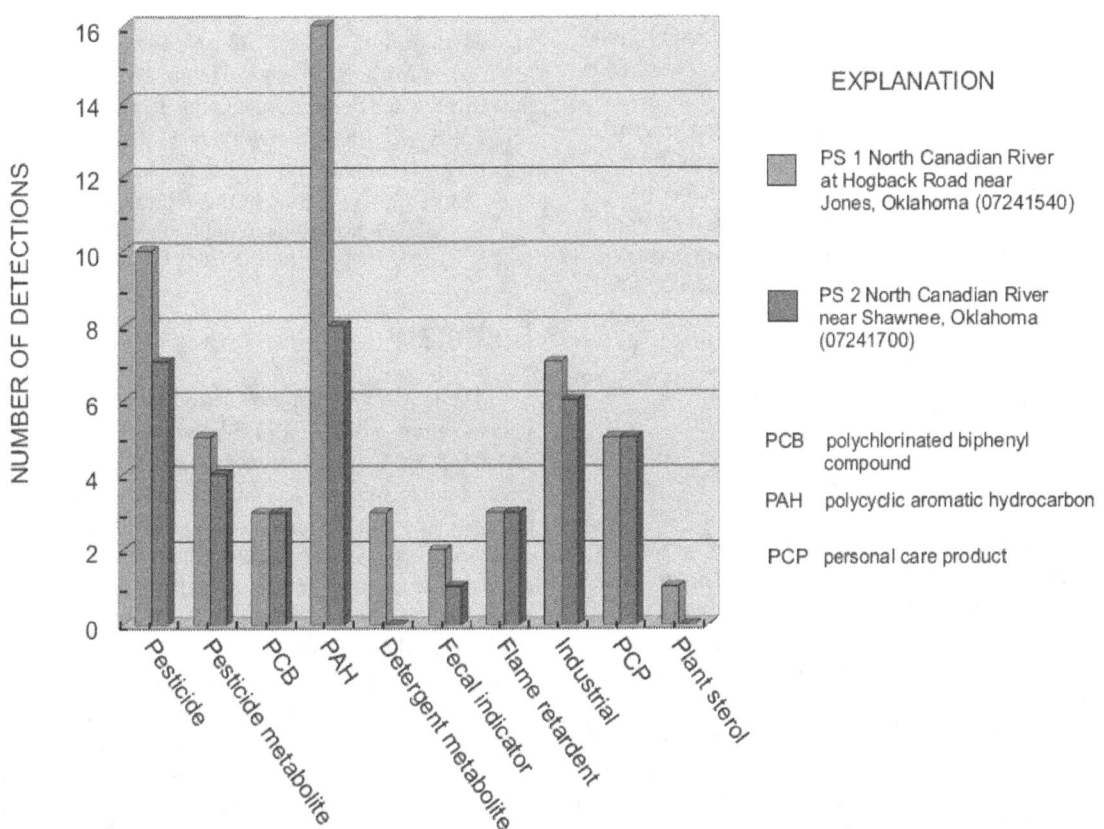

Figure 5. The number of detections of pesticides, pesticide metabolites, polychlorinated biphenyl compounds, polycyclic aromatic hydrocarbons, and other types of synthetic organic compounds measured in extracts from Semipermeable Membrane Devices or Polar Organic Integrative Samplers submerged at two stream sites on the North Canadian River adjacent to the Kickapoo tribal lands in central Oklahoma, January–February 2009.

Polychlorinated Biphenyl Compounds and Polycyclic Aromatic Hydrocarbons

Sites PS-1 and PS-2, had detections of the PCB compounds aroclor-1016/1242, aroclor-1254, and aroclor-1260. PCBs were used in many types of industrial applications, such as plasticizers, flame retardants, sealants, dielectric fluids, and adhesives (U.S. Environmental Protection Agency, 2009a). PCBs were banned in 1976, but are still found throughout the environment, as these compounds are persistent and attenuate slowly. The MCL for PCB compounds in drinking water is 5,000 ng/L. The sum of those three compound concentrations approximated in stream water at PS-1 and PS-2 is small, less than 6 ng/L.

PAHs compose a large group of organic compounds that are formed by the incomplete combustion of coal, oil, gas, wood, and other organic substances and are found in the environment in soil, water, or air attached to particulates. Selected PAHs are used in the manufacture of explosives and mothballs, are found in cigarette smoke, and are used in cancer research (U.S. Environmental Protection Agency, 1995).

Site PS-1 had 16 PAH detections and PS-2 had 8 detections of the 35 PAHs analyzed. Because of chromatographic interference during analysis, a positive identification of 17 PAHs in extracts from PS-1 and 18 in PS-2 could not be made. Consequently, there may have been a greater number of PAH compounds in extracts from these two sites.

Five PAHs only detected at PS-1, benzo(a)anthracene, benzo(b)fluoranthene, benzo(ghi)perylene, benzo(k)fluoranthene, and chrysene, are considered to have endocrine disruption potential (Kegley and others, 2008) and except for benzo(ghi)perylene, are considered probable human carcinogens by the U.S. Environmental Protection Agency (2002a). Fluoranthene and pyrene had the largest approximate concentrations in water of the PAHs detected at PS-1 (12.6 and 12.3 ng/L) and at PS-2 (6.12 and 5.11 ng/L), respectively. None of the detected PAHs have MCLs for drinking water.

Synthetic Organic Compounds

SOCs were grouped into five categories on the basis of a common use of the compound; detergent metabolite, fecal indicator, flame retardant, industrial compound, and PCP (fig. 5). Seven SOCs were categorized as industrial because these compounds are used in the manufacture of many types of products, such as pentachloroanisol, which is used in the manufacture of polymers, pesticides, and fire retardants and is also used as a wood preservative. The compound beta-sitosterol is a natural plant sterol and also is used as a vitamin supplement. This compound was detected at PS-1; however, because the compound is natural, it was not included in the five compound use groups.

Similar to the PAHs, chromatographic interference during laboratory analysis affected the positive identification of SOCs in extracts from both sites. Consequently, the presence of 12

SOCs from PS-1 and 4 SOCs from PS-2 could not be determined. An additional eight SOCs in extracts from PS-2 could not be positively identified most likely because of isopropanol residue from the addition of spike and surrogate solution during the analytical procedure (Duane Wydoski, U.S. Geological Survey, National Water Quality Laboratory, personal commun., 2009)

Sample site PS-1 had 21 SOC detections: 3 detergent metabolites, 2 fecal indicators, 3 flame retardants, 7 industrial compounds, 5 PCPs, and beta-sitosterol (fig. 5). Three detergent metabolites p-nonylphenol, 4-tert-octylphenol diethoxylate, and triclosan; two flame retardants tri(2-chloroethyl) phosphate, and tri(dichlorisopropyl)phosphate; the industrial compound pentachloroanisole, and three PCPs, benzophenone, galaxolide, and tonalide are suspected or are known to be endocrine disruptors.

The 15 SOCs detected at PS-2, downstream from PS-1, were a subset of the 21 detected at PS-1 and included 1 fecal indicator, 3 flame retardants, 6 industrial compounds, and 5 PCPs. Two of the flame retardants, tri(2-chloroethyl) phosphate and tri(dichlorisopropyl)phosphate; the industrial compound pentachloroanisole and three PCPs, benzophenone, galaxolide, and tonalide are suspected or known to be endocrine disruptors.

Three SOCs having the largest measured concentrations in extracts from PS-1 and PS-2 were 5-methyl-1H-benzotriazole (an antirust and corrosion inhibitor and an antioxidant in antifreeze and deicers), galaxolide (a musk fragrance), and tri(2-butoxyethyl)phosphate (a flame retardant). Galaxolide is the only compound of the three that is known to be an endocrine disruptor. At the time of this report (2010), none of the detected SOCs have MCLs in public drinking-water supplies.

Summary

The USGS Oklahoma Water Science Center worked in cooperation with the US EPA and the Kickapoo Tribe of Oklahoma on two separate reconnaissance projects carried out concurrently. Both projects entailed the use of passive samplers as a sampling methodology to investigate the detection of selected organic compounds at stream sites in jurisdictional areas of several tribes in central Oklahoma during January–February 2009.

In cooperation with the Kickapoo Tribe of Oklahoma, SPMDs and POCIS were submerged at two sites; one at the upstream western edge (PS-1) and the other at the downstream eastern edge (PS-2) of the Kickapoo tribal boundaries. Both sites are downstream from the Oklahoma City metropolitan area and multiple wastewater treatment plants. Extract composites were analyzed for 62 pesticides, 10 pesticide metabolites, 3 PCBs compounds, 35 PAHs, and 49 SOCs.

Ten pesticides and four pesticide metabolites were detected at the upstream site (PS-1) and seven pesticides and four pesticide metabolites, of 62 pesticides analyzed, were detected at the downstream site (PS-2). Pesticides detected at both sites were the herbicides atrazine, dacthal, metolachlor, pendimethalin, and the insecticides chlorpyrifos, dieldrin, and trans-nonachlor. Pesticide metabolites detected at both sites were p,p'-DDE, and cis-chlordane and trans-chlordane, both pesticide metabolites of the legacy insecticide chlordane. Additionally at the upstream site, the herbicides pentachlorophenol, prometon, and the insecticide heptachlor were detected.

Concentrations of three detected pesticides and one metabolite are regulated in public-drinking water by the US EPA with maximum contaminant levels of atrazine (3,000 ng/L), heptachlor (400 ng/L), heptachlor epoxide (200 ng/L), and pentachlorophenol (1,000 ng/L). However, the approximate water concentrations of heptachlor and heptachlor epoxide representing stream samples are small, about 2,000 to 4,000 times smaller than the respective maximum contaminant levels in drinking water. The water concentrations of atrazine and pentachlorophenol could not be calculated because these compounds were measured in POCIS extracts.

The PCB compounds aroclor-1016/1242, aroclor-1254, and aroclor-1260 were detected at both sites. The maximum contaminant level for PCBs in drinking water is 5,000 ng/L. The sum of the three compound concentrations approximated in stream water is small, less than 6 ng/L.

The upstream site PS-1 had 16 PAH detections and the downstream site PS-2 had eight detections. Because of chromatographic interference during analysis, a positive identification of 17 PAHs could not be made. Consequently, there may have been a greater number of these compounds in extracts from the two sites. None of the detected PAHs have maximum contaminant levels for public drinking-water supplies.

A total of 36 SOCs were detected at the two sites adjacent to the Kickapoo tribal lands. The upstream site PS-1 had 21 SOC detections; three detergent metabolites, two fecal indicators, three flame retardants, seven industrial compounds, and five compounds related to personal care products. Beta-sitosterol also was detected. Fifteen SOCs were detected at the downstream site PS-2 and included; one fecal indicator, three flame retardants, six industrial compounds, and five compounds related to personal care products. Similar to the PAHs, chromatographic interference during laboratory analysis affected the positive identification of SOCs in extracts from both sites. Consequently, the presence of 12 SOCs at site PS-1 and four at site PS-2 could not be determined. An additional eight SOCs in extracts from the downstream site could not be positively identified most likely because of isopropanol residue from the addition of spike and surrogate solution during the analytical procedure.

Three SOCs having the largest measured concentrations in extracts from PS-1 and PS-2 were 5-methyl-1H-benzotriazole (an antirust and corrosion inhibitor and an antioxidant in antifreeze and deicers), galaxolide a musk fragrance, and tri(2-butoxyethyl)phosphate a flame retardant. Galaxolide is the only compound of the three that is known to be an endocrine disruptor. At the time of this report, none of the detected SOCs have maximum contaminant levels in public drinking-water supplies.

In cooperation with the US EPA, SPMDs were submerged at five stream sites located at USGS stream-gaging stations on the Cimarron River, Little River, North Canadian River, Deep Fork, and the Washita River. A composite of extracts from three SPMDs submerged at each site was analyzed for 46 pesticides and 6 pesticide metabolites. Dacthal a pre-emergent herbicide was detected at all five sites. Pendimethalin also a pre-emergent was detected at one site. The insecticides chlorpyrifos and dieldrin were detected at three sites and p,p'-DDE a metabolite of the insecticide DDT also was detected at three sites.

References Cited

Alvarez, D.A., Petty, J.D., Huckins, J.N., Jones-Lepp, T.L., Getting, D.T., Goddard, J.P., and Manahan, S.E., 2004, Development of a passive, in situ, integrative sampler for hydrophilic organic contaminants in aquatic environments: Environmental Toxicology and Chemistry, v. 23, no. 7, p. 1,640–1,648.

Brigham, Mark E., Payne, Gregory A., Andrews, William J., 2002, Statistical analysis of stream water-quality data and sampling network design near Oklahoma City, central Oklahoma, 1977–1999; U.S. Geological Survey Water-Resources Investigations Report 02–4111, 24 p.

Crain, A.D., Janssen, S.J., Edwards, T.M., Heindel, Jerrold, Ho, Shuk-mei, Hunt, Patricia, Iguchi, Taisen, Juul, Anders, McLachlan, J.A., Schwartz, Jackie, Skakkebaek, Niels, Soto, A.M., Swan, Shanna, Walker, Cheryl, Woodruff, T.K., Woodruff, T.J., Giudice, L.C., and Guillette, Louis, Jr., 2008, Female reproductive disorders—The roles of endocrine-disrupting compounds and developmental timing: Fertility and Sterility, v. 90, no. 4, p. 911–940.

Dean, John R., 2010, Extraction techniques in analytical sciences, Chapter 1, Pre- and post-extraction considerations: West Sussex, United Kingdom, John Wiley & Sons, Ltd, 277 p.

Environmental Sampling Technologies, 2008, Product—Semipermeable Membrane Device (SPMD) and its deployment, available online at *http://www.est-lab.com/spmd.php*. (Accessed March 28, 2008.)

Galloway, J.M., Haggard, B.E., Meyer, M.T., and Green, W.R., 2004, Occurrence of pharmaceuticals and other organic wastewater constituents in selected streams in northern Arkansas, 2004: U.S. Geological Survey Scientific Investigations Report 2005–5140, 24 p. (Also available online at *http://pubs.usgs.gov/sir/2005/5140/SIR2005-5140.pdf*.)

Gilliom, Robert J., and others, 2006, The quality of our Nation's waters—Pesticides in the Nation's streams and ground water, 1992–2001: U.S. Geological Survey Circular 1291, 173 p. (Also available online at *http://pubs.usgs.gov/circ/2005/1291/.*)

Huckins, J.N., Petty, J.D., and Booij, Kees, 2006, Monitors of organic chemicals in the environment—Semipermeable Membrane Devices: New York, Springer Science+Business Media, 223 p.

Kegley, S.E., Hill, B.R., Orme, S., and Choi, A.H., 2008, PAN Pesticide Database, Pesticide Action Network, North America, available online at *http:www.pesticideinfo.org.* (Accessed September 9, 2009.)

Kolpin, D.W., Furlong, E.T., Meyer, M.T., Thurman, E.M., Zaugg, S.D., Barber, L.B, and Buxton, H.T., 2002, Pharmaceuticals, hormones, and other organic wastewater contaminants in U.S. streams, 1999–2000—A national reconnaissance: Environmental Science and Technology v. 36, no. 6, p. 1,202–1,211.

Kolpin, D.W., Sneck-Fahrer, D.A., Hallberg, G.R., and Libra, R.D., 1997, Temporal trends of selected agricultural chemicals in Iowa's groundwater, 1982–95—Are things getting better?: Journal of Environmental Quality, v. 26, no. 4, p. 1,007–1,017.

Masoner, J.R., and Mashburn, S.L., 2004, Water quality and possible sources of nitrate in the Cimarron Terrace aquifer, Oklahoma, 2003: U.S. Geological Survey Scientific Investigations Report 2004–5221, 60 p.

Noriega, M.C., Wydoski, D.S., and Foreman, W.T., 2004, Methods of analysis by the U.S. Geological Survey National Water Quality Laboratory—Determination of organochlorine pesticides and polychlorinated biphenyls in bottom and suspended sediment by gas chromatography with electron-capture detection: U.S. Geological Survey Water-Resources Investigations Report 03–4293, 46 p. (Also available online at *http://nwql.usgs.gov/Public/pubs/WRIR03-4293/WRIR03-4293.pdf.*)

Oklahoma Department of Environmental Quality, 2009, GIS data viewer, NPDES Outfalls, data collected online at *http://maps.scigis.com/deq_wq/.* (Accessed September 9, 2008.)

Rhomberg, Lorenz, and Seeley, Mara, 2005, Environmental hormone disruptors: Encyclopedia of Toxicology (2d ed.), Elsevier, Inc., p. 205–208.

Tertuliani, J.S., Alvarez, D.A., Furlong, E.T., Meyer, M.T., Zaugg, S.D., and Koltun, G.F., 2008, Occurrence of organic wastewater compounds in the Tinkers Creek watershed and two other tributaries to the Cuyahoga River, northeast Ohio: U.S. Geological Survey Scientific Investigations Report 2008–5173, 60 p.

Tulane and Xavier Universities, Center for Bioenvironmental Research, 2009a, Endocrine disrupting chemicals—Altered states, available online at *http://e.hormone.tulane.edu/learning/endocrine-disrupting-chemicals.html.* (Accessed August 29, 2009.)

Tulane and Xavier Universities, Center for Bioenvironmental Research, 2009b, Endocrine disrupting chemicals—Human effects, available online at *http://e.hormone.tulane.edu/learning/human-effects.html.* (Accessed August 29, 2009.)

U.S. Department of Labor, Occupational Safety and Health Administration, 2009, Chemical sampling information, available online at *http://www.osha.gov/dts/chemicalsampling/toc/toc_chemsamp.html.* (Accessed September 9, 2008.)

U.S. Environmental Protection Agency, 1995, Public health statement for polycyclic aromatic hydrocarbons (PAHs), available on line at, *http://www.atsdr.cdc.gov/toxprofiles/phs69.html.* (Accessed December 22, 2009.)

U.S. Environmental Protection Agency, 2001, National Land Cover Data—Multi-Resolution Land Characteristics Consortium, available online at *http://www.epa.gov/mrlc/nlcd-2001.html.* (Accessed September 9, 2008.)

U.S. Environmental Protection Agency, 2002a, Peer consultation workshop on approaches to polycyclic aromatic hydrocarbon (PAH) health assessment: National Center for Environmental Assessment, U.S. Environmental Protection Agency, EPA/635/R-02/005, available online at *http://cfpub.epa.gov/ncea/cfm/recordisplay.cfm?deid=54787.* (Accessed January 12, 2009.)

U.S. Environmental Protection Agency, 2002b, Chlorpyrifos facts: EPA 738-F-01-006, available online at *http://www.epa.gov/pesticides/reregistration/REDs/factsheets/chlorpyrifos_fs.htm.* (Accessed January 12, 2009.)

U.S. Environmental Protection Agency, 2009a, Drinking water contaminants, organic chemicals, available online at *http://www.epa.gov/safewater/contaminants/index.html#organic.* (Accessed January 12, 2009.)

U.S. Environmental Protection Agency, 2009b, Basic information about polychlorinated biphenyls (PCBs) in drinking water; *http://www.epa.gov/safewater/contaminants/basicinformation/polychlorinated-biphenyls.html.* (Accessed January 4, 2010.)

U.S. Geological Survey, Columbia Environmental Research Center, 2004, Polar Organic Chemical Integrative Sampler (POCIS), available on online at *http://www.cerc.usgs.gov/pubs/center/pdfDSOCs/POCIS.pdf.* (Accessed March 12, 2009.)

U.S. Geological Survey, Columbia Environmental Research Center, 2006, Estimated water concentration calculator from SPMD data using PRCs, SPMD calculator version 5, updated November 15, 2006, available online at *http://www.*

cerc.usgs.gov/Branches.aspx?BranchId=8. (Accessed January 12, 2009.)

Zaugg, S.D., Burkhardt, M.R., Burbank, T.L., Olson, M.C., Iverson, J.L., and Schroeder, M.P., 2006, Determination of semivolatile organic compounds and polycyclic aromatic hydrocarbons in solids by gas chromatography/mass spectrometry, Method ID: O-5506-06: U.S. Geological Survey Techniques and Methods, book 5, chap. B3, 44 p. (Also available online at *http://pubs.usgs.gov/tm/2006/tm5b3/.*)

Zaugg, S.D., Sandstrom, M.W., Smith, S.G., and Fehlberg, K.M., 1995, Methods of analysis by the U.S. Geological Survey National Water Quality Laboratory—Determination of pesticides in water by C-18 solid-phase extraction and capillary-column gas chromatography/mass spectrometry with selected-ion monitoring, Method ID: O-1126-95: U.S. Geological Survey Open-File Report 95–181, 49 p. (Also available online at *http://nwql.usgs.gov/Public/pubs/OFR95_181.pdf.*)

Zaugg, S.D., Smith, S.G., Schroeder, M.P., Barber, L.B., and Burkhardt, M.R., 2007, Methods of analysis by the U.S. Geological Survey National Water Quality Laboratory—Determination of wastewater compounds by polystyrene-divinylbenzene solid-phase extraction and capillary-column gas chromatography/mass spectrometry: U.S. Geological Survey Water-Resources Investigations Report 01–4186, 37 p. [revised].

Appendix 1—Organic Compounds

Appendix 1. Organic compounds as analyzed in extracts from Semipermeable Membrane Devices or Polar Organic Chemical Integrative Samplers for this study, including suspected endocrine disruption potential, Chemical Abstract Service number, possible compound uses or sources (modified from Zaugg and others [2007] and Tertuliani and others [2008]), sampler type used to sequester compound, and laboratory method used for analysis.

[EDC, known or suspected endocrine disruptor; -, no or status is not known; na, not available; CAS, Chemical Abstract Service; PAH, polycyclic aromatic hydrocarbon; US EPA, U.S. Environmental Protection Agency; SPMD, Semipermeable Membrane Device; Polar Organic Chemical Integrative Sampler, POCIS]

Compound	EDC[1,2,3]	CAS number[6]	Possible compound uses or sources[1,2,3,4,5]	Sampler type	Laboratory method
1-Methylnaphthalene	-	90-12-0	PAH, used in the manufacture of dyes, plastics, and resins	POCIS	Zaugg and others (2007)
1-Methyl-9H-fluorene	-	1730-37-6	PAH	SPMD	Zaugg and others (2006)
1-Methylphenanthrene	-	832-69-9	PAH	SPMD	Zaugg and others (2006)
1-Methylpyrene	-	2381-21-7	PAH	SPMD	Zaugg and others (2006)
1,2,4-Trichlorobenzene	-	120-82-1	PAH	SPMD	Zaugg and others (2006)
1,2-Dimethylnaphthalene	-	573-98-8	PAH	SPMD	Zaugg and others (2006)
1,4-Dichlorobenzene	Yes	106-46-7	Moth repellant, fumigant, deodorant	POCIS	Zaugg and others (2007)
1,6-Dimethylnaphthalene	-	575-43-9	PAH	SPMD	Zaugg and others (2006)
2-Ethylnaphthalene	-	939-27-5	PAH	SPMD	Zaugg and others (2006)
2-Methylanthracene	-	613-12-7	PAH	SPMD	Zaugg and others (2006)
2-Methylnaphthalene	-	91-57-6	PAH	POCIS	Zaugg and others (2007)
2,3,6-Trimethylnaphthalene	-	829-26-5	PAH	SPMD	Zaugg and others (2006)
2,6-Diethylaniline	-	579-66-8	Used in the production of triazine herbicides	SPMD	Zaugg and others (1995)
2,6-Dimethylnaphthalene	-	581-42-0	PAH, present in diesel/kerosene (trace in gasoline)	SPMD, POCIS	Zaugg and others (2006; 2007)
3-beta-Coprostanol	-	360-68-9	Carnivore fecal indicator	POCIS	Zaugg and others (2007)
3-methyl-1(H)-indole (Skatol)	-	83-34-1	Stench in feces, present in coal tar	POCIS	Zaugg and others (2007)
3-tert-Butyl-4-hydroxyanisole (BHA)	Yes	25013-16-5	Antioxidant, general preservative	POCIS	Zaugg and others (2007)
4-Cumylphenol	Yes	599-64-4	Nonionic detergent metabolite	POCIS	Zaugg and others (2007)
4-n-Octylphenol	Yes	1806-26-4	Nonionic detergent metabolite	POCIS	Zaugg and others (2007)
4-Nonylphenol diethoxylate (NP2EO; total)	Yes	na	Nonionic detergent metabolite	POCIS	Zaugg and others (2007)
4-Nonylphenol monoethoxylate (NP1EO)	Yes	104-35-8	Nonionic detergent metabolite	POCIS	Zaugg and others (2007)
4-tert-Octylphenol diethoxylate (OP2EO)	Yes	na	Nonionic detergent metabolite	POCIS	Zaugg and others (2007)
4-tert-Octylphenol monoethoxylate (OP1EO; total)	Yes	na	Nonionic detergent metabolite	POCIS	Zaugg and others (2007)
4-tert-Octylphenol	Yes	140-66-9	Nonionic detergent metabolite	POCIS	Zaugg and others (2007)
4,5-Methylenephenanthrene	-	203-64-5	PAH	SPMD	Zaugg and others (2006)

Appendix 1.   Organic compounds as analyzed in extracts from Semipermeable Membrane Devices or Polar Organic Chemical Integrative Samplers for this study, including suspected endocrine disruption potential, Chemical Abstract Service number, possible compound uses or sources (modified from Zaugg and others [2007] and Tertuliani and others [2008]), sampler type used to sequester compound, and laboratory method used for analysis.—Continued

[EDC, known or suspected endocrine disruptor; -, no or status is not known; na, not available; CAS, Chemical Abstract Service; PAH, polycyclic aromatic hydrocarbon; US EPA, U.S. Environmental Protection Agency; SPMD, Semipermeable Membrane Device; Polar Organic Chemical Integrative Sampler, POCIS]

Compound	EDC[1,2,3]	CAS number[6]	Possible compound uses or sources[1,2,3,4,5]	Sampler type	Laboratory method
5-methyl-1H-benzotriazole	-	136-85-6	Antirust and corrosion inhibitor, anti-oxidant in antifreeze and deicers	POCIS	Zaugg and others (2007)
Acenaphthene	-	83-32-9	PAH	SPMD	Zaugg and others (2006)
Acenaphthylene	-	208-96-8	PAH, used in dye synthesis, insecticides, fungicides, and in the manufacture of plastics	SPMD	Zaugg and others (2006)
Acetochlor	Yes	34256-82-1	Herbicide	SPMD	Zaugg and others (1995)
Alachlor	Yes	15972-60-8	Herbicide, regulated in drinking water by the US EPA	SPMD	Zaugg and others (1995)
Acetophenone	-	98-86-2	Fragrance in detergent and tobacco, flavor in beverages	POCIS	Zaugg and others (2007)
Aldrin	Yes	309-00-2	Organochlorine pesticide, banned in 1987, degrades to dieldrin	SPMD	Noriega and others (2004)
alpha-Endosulfan	Yes	959-98-8	Insecticide	SPMD	Noriega and others (2004)
alpha-Hexachlorocyclohex-ane (BHC)	-	319-84-6	Insecticide	SPMD	Noriega and others (2004), Zaugg and others (1995)
Anthracene	-	120-12-7	PAH, wood preservative	SPMD	Zaugg and others (2006; 2007)
Anthraquinone	-	84-65-1	PAH, dye manufacture and textiles, seed treatment, bird repellant	SPMD	Zaugg and others (2006; 2007)
Aroclor 1016/1242	-	na	A polychlorinated biphenyl compound used in industrial processes	SPMD	Noriega and others (2004)
Aroclor 1254	Yes	11097-69-1	A polychlorinated biphenyl compound used in industrial processes	SPMD	Noriega and others (2004)
Aroclor 1260	-	11096-82-5	A polychlorinated biphenyl compound used in industrial processes	SPMD	Noriega and others (2004)
Atrazine	Yes	1912-24-9	Herbicide, regulated in drinking water by the US EPA	SPMD	Zaugg and others (1995; 2007)
Benfluralin	-	1861-40-1	Herbicide	SPMD	Zaugg and others (1995)
Benzo(a)anthracene	Yes	56-55-3	PAH, probable human carcinogen	SPMD	Zaugg and others (2006)
Benzo(b)fluoranthene	Yes	205-99-2	PAH, probable human carcinogen	SPMD	Zaugg and others (2006)
Benzo(a)pyrene	Yes	50-32-8	PAH, probable human carcinogen, used in cancer research, combustion product, found in cigarette smoke, regulated in drinking water by the US EPA	SPMD	Zaugg and others (2006; 2007)
Benzo(e)pyrene	-	192-97-2	PAH	SPMD	Zaugg and others (2006)
Benzo(ghi)perylene	Yes	191-24-2	PAH	SPMD	Zaugg and others (2006)
Benzo(k)fluoranthene	Yes	207-08-9	PAH, probable human carcinogen	SPMD	Zaugg and others (2006)

Appendix 1.   Organic compounds as analyzed in extracts from Semipermeable Membrane Devices or Polar Organic Chemical Integrative Samplers for this study, including suspected endocrine disruption potential, Chemical Abstract Service number, possible compound uses or sources (modified from Zaugg and others [2007] and Tertuliani and others [2008]), sampler type used to sequester compound, and laboratory method used for analysis.—Continued

[EDC, known or suspected endocrine disruptor; -, no or status is not known; na, not available; CAS, Chemical Abstract Service; PAH, polycyclic aromatic hydrocarbon; US EPA, U.S. Environmental Protection Agency; SPMD, Semipermeable Membrane Device; Polar Organic Chemical Integrative Sampler, POCIS]

Compound	EDC[1,2,3]	CAS number[6]	Possible compound uses or sources[1,2,3,4,5]	Sampler type	Laboratory method
Benzophenone	Yes	119-61-9	Ultra violet blocker in perfumes, soaps, and plastics	POCIS	Zaugg and others (2007)
beta-Hexachlorobenzene	Yes	319-85-7	Insecticide	SPMD	Noriega and others (2004)
beta-Sitosterol	-	83-46-5	Plant sterol	POCIS	Zaugg and others (2007)
beta-Stigmastanol	-	19466-47-8	Plant sterol	POCIS	Zaugg and others (2007)
Bisphenol A	Yes	80-05-7	Plasticizer, manufacture of polycarbonate resins, antioxidant, fire repellant	POCIS	Zaugg and others (2007)
Bromacil	-	314-40-9	General use herbicide	POCIS	Zaugg and others (2007)
Bromoform	-	75-25-2	Wastewater ozonation byproduct, military/explosives	POCIS	Zaugg and others (2007)
Butylate	-	2008-41-5	Herbicide	SPMD	Zaugg and others (1995)
Caffeine	-	58-08-2	Beverages, diuretic, very mobile and biodegradable	POCIS	Zaugg and others (2007)
Camphor	-	76-22-2	Flavor, odorant, ointments	POCIS	Zaugg and others (2007)
Carbaryl	Yes	63-25-2	Insecticide, crop and garden uses, low persistence	SPMD	Zaugg and others (1995; 2007)
Carbazole	-	86-74-8	PAH, insecticide, manufacture of dyes, explosives, and lubricants	SPMD	Zaugg and others (2006)
Carbofuran	Yes	1563-66-2	Insecticide	SPMD	Zaugg and others (1995)
cis-Chlordane	Yes	5103-71-9	Chlordane metabolite, banned, considered a legacy pesticide	SPMD	Noriega and others (2004)
trans-Chlordane	Yes	5103-74-2	Chlordane metabolite, banned, considered a legacy pesticide	SPMD	Noriega and others (2004)
Chlorpyrifos	Yes	2921-88-2	Insecticide, residential use restricted as of 2001, common name is dursban	SPMD, POCIS	Zaugg and others (1995; 2007)
Cholesterol	-	57-88-5	Often a fecal indicator, also a plant sterol	POCIS	Zaugg and others (2007)
Chrysene	Yes	218-01-9	PAH, probable human carcinogen	SPMD	Zaugg and others (2006)
Cotinine	-	486-56-6	Metabolite of nicotine	POCIS	Zaugg and others (2007)
Cumene (Isopropylbenzene)	-	98-82-8	Manufacture phenol/acetone, fuels and paint thinner	POCIS	Zaugg and others (2007)
Cyanazine	Yes	21725-46-2	Herbicide	SPMD	Zaugg and others (1995)
Dacthal	-	1861-32-1	Pre-emergent herbicide	SPMD	Zaugg and others (1995)
Deethylatrazine	-	6190-65-4	Metabolite of atrazine	SPMD	Zaugg and others (1995)
Desulfinylfipronil	-	na	Metabolite of fipronil	SPMD	Zaugg and others (1995)

Appendix 1. Organic compounds as analyzed in extracts from Semipermeable Membrane Devices or Polar Organic Chemical Integrative Samplers for this study, including suspected endocrine disruption potential, Chemical Abstract Service number, possible compound uses or sources (modified from Zaugg and others [2007] and Tertuliani and others [2008]), sampler type used to sequester compound, and laboratory method used for analysis.—Continued

[EDC, known or suspected endocrine disruptor; -, no or status is not known; na, not available; CAS, Chemical Abstract Service; PAH, polycyclic aromatic hydrocarbon; US EPA, U.S. Environmental Protection Agency; SPMD, Semipermeable Membrane Device; Polar Organic Chemical Integrative Sampler, POCIS]

Compound	EDC[1,2,3]	CAS number[6]	Possible compound uses or sources[1,2,3,4,5]	Sampler type	Laboratory method
Desulfinylfipronil amide	-	na	Metabolite of fipronil	SPMD	Zaugg and others (1995)
Diazinon	Yes	333-41-5	Insecticide, residential use banned in 2004	SPMD	Zaugg and others (1995), Zaugg and others (2007)
Dibenz(ah)anthracene	Yes	53-70-3	PAH, probable human carcinogen	SPMD	Zaugg and others (2006)
Dibenzothiophene	-	132-65-0	PAH, present in petroleum products	SPMD	Zaugg and others (2006)
Dieldrin	Yes	60-57-1	Insecticide, banned in 1987, considered a legacy pesticide	SPMD	Noriega and others (2004), Zaugg and others (1995)
bis(2-ethylhexyl)phthalate	Yes	117-81-7	Plasticizer for polymers and resins, inert ingredient in pesticides	SPMD	Zaugg and others (2006)
Diethylphthalate	Yes	84-66-2	Plasticizer for polymers and resins	SPMD	Zaugg and others (2006)
Disulfoton	-	298-04-4	Insecticide	SPMD	Zaugg and others (1995)
d-Limonene	-	5989-27-5	Fragrance, cleaning products	POCIS	Zaugg and others (2007)
Endrin	Yes	72-20-8	Insecticide, banned, considered a legacy pesticide, regulated in drinking water by the US EPA	SPMD	Noriega and others (2004)
Eptam (EPTC)	-	759-94-4	Herbicide	SPMD	Zaugg and others (1995)
Ethyl citrate	-	77-93-0	Solvent, used in paints and perfumes, used to decaffeinate coffee and tea	POCIS	Zaugg and others (2007)
Ethalfluralin	-	55283-68-6	Herbicide	SPMD	Zaugg and others (1995)
Ethoprop	-	13194-48-4	Insecticide	SPMD	Zaugg and others (1995)
Fipronil	Yes	120068-37-3	Insecticide	SPMD	Zaugg and others (1995)
Fipronil sulfide	-	120067-83-6	Metabolite of fipronil	SPMD	Zaugg and others (1995)
Fipronil sulfone	-	120068-36-2	Metabolite of fipronil	SPMD	Zaugg and others (1995)
Fluoranthene	-	206-44-0	PAH, component of coal tar and asphalt, traces in gasoline and diesel fuel	SPMD, POCIS	Zaugg and others (2006; 2007)
Fluorene	-	86-73-7	PAH, occurs in coal tar	SPMD	Zaugg and others (2006)
Fonofos	-	944-22-9	Insecticide	SPMD	Zaugg and others (1995)
Galaxolide (HHCB)	Yes	1222-05-5	Musk fragrance, persistent and widespread in ground water, concern for bioaccumulation and toxicity	POCIS	Zaugg and others (2007)
Heptachlor	Yes	76-44-8	Insecticide, banned in 1974, used as a termaticide under certain circumstances	SPMD	Noriega and others (2004)
Heptachlor epoxide	Yes	1024-57-3	Metabolite of heptachlor	SPMD	Noriega and others (2004)

Appendix 1.   Organic compounds as analyzed in extracts from Semipermeable Membrane Devices or Polar Organic Chemical Integrative Samplers for this study, including suspected endocrine disruption potential, Chemical Abstract Service number, possible compound uses or sources (modified from Zaugg and others [2007] and Tertuliani and others [2008]), sampler type used to sequester compound, and laboratory method used for analysis.—Continued

[EDC, known or suspected endocrine disruptor; -, no or status is not known; na, not available; CAS, Chemical Abstract Service; PAH, polycyclic aromatic hydrocarbon; US EPA, U.S. Environmental Protection Agency; SPMD, Semipermeable Membrane Device; Polar Organic Chemical Integrative Sampler, POCIS]

Compound	EDC[1,2,3]	CAS number[6]	Possible compound uses or sources[1,2,3,4,5]	Sampler type	Laboratory method
Hexachlorobenzene	Yes	118-74-1	Fungicide, carcinogen, banned from use	SPMD	Noriega and others (2004), Zaugg and others (2006)
Indeno(1,2,3-cd)pyrene	Yes	193-39-5	PAH, probable human carcinogen	SPMD	Zaugg and others (2006)
Indole	-	120-72-9	Pesticide inert ingredient, fragrance in coffee, stench in feces	POCIS	Zaugg and others (2007)
Isoborneol	-	124-76-5	Fragrance	POCIS	Zaugg and others (2007)
Isophorone	-	78-59-1	Solvent for lacquer, plastic, oil, silicon, resin	POCIS	Zaugg and others (2007)
Isoquinoline	-	119-65-3	Flavors and fragrances	POCIS	Zaugg and others (2007)
Lindane	Yes	58-89-9	Insecticide, banned in 2009	SPMD	Zaugg and others (1995), Noriega and others (2004)
Linuron	Yes	330-55-2	Herbicide	SPMD	Zaugg and others (1995)
Malathion	Yes	121-75-5	Insecticide	SPMD	Zaugg and others (1995)
Menthol	-	89-78-1	Liniment, cigarettes, cough drops, mouthwash	POCIS	Zaugg and others (2007)
Metalaxyl	-	57837-19-1	Fungicide	POCIS	Zaugg and others (2007)
Methyl azinphos	-	86-50-0	Insecticide	SPMD	Zaugg and others (1995)
Methyl parathion	Yes	298-00-0	Insecticide	SPMD	Zaugg and others (1995)
Methyl salicylate	-	119-36-8	Liniment, food, beverage, ultra violet-absorbing lotion	POCIS	Zaugg and others (2007)
Metolachlor	-	51218-45-2	Herbicide, general use pesticide, indicator of agricultural drainage	SPMD	Zaugg and others (1995; 2007)
Metribuzin	Yes	21087-64-9	Herbicide	SPMD	Zaugg and others (1995)
Mirex	Yes	2358-85-5	Insecticide	SPMD	Noriega and others (2004)
Molinate	Yes	2212-67-1	Herbicide	SPMD	Zaugg and others (1995)
Napropamide	-	15299-99-7	Herbicide	SPMD	Zaugg and others (1995)
N,N-diethyl-meta-toluamide (DEET)	-	134-62-3	Insecticide, urban uses, mosquito repellent	POCIS	Zaugg and others (2007)
Naphthalene	-	91-20-3	PAH, fumigant, moth repellent	SPMD	Zaugg and others (2006; 2007)
p-Cresol	-	106-44-5	Wood preservative	POCIS	Zaugg and others (2007)
p-Nonylphenol (total)	Yes	84852-15-3	Nonionic detergent metabolite	POCIS	Zaugg and others (2007)
p,p'-DDD	Yes	72-54-8	Metabolite of DDT	SPMD	Noriega and others (2004)
p,p'-DDE	Yes	72-55-9	Metabolite of DDT	SPMD	Noriega and others (2004), Zaugg and others (1995)

Appendix 1.   Organic compounds as analyzed in extracts from Semipermeable Membrane Devices or Polar Organic Chemical Integrative Samplers for this study, including suspected endocrine disruption potential, Chemical Abstract Service number, possible compound uses or sources (modified from Zaugg and others [2007] and Tertuliani and others [2008]), sampler type used to sequester compound, and laboratory method used for analysis.—Continued

[EDC, known or suspected endocrine disruptor; -, no or status is not known; na, not available; CAS, Chemical Abstract Service; PAH, polycyclic aromatic hydrocarbon; US EPA, U.S. Environmental Protection Agency; SPMD, Semipermeable Membrane Device; Polar Organic Chemical Integrative Sampler, POCIS]

Compound	EDC[1,2,3]	CAS number[6]	Possible compound uses or sources[1,2,3,4,5]	Sampler type	Laboratory method
p,p'-DDT	Yes	50-29-3	Insecticide, considered a legacy pesticide, banned in 1972	SPMD	Noriega and others (2004)
p,p'-Methoxychlor	Yes	72-43-5	Insecticide	SPMD	Noriega and others (2004)
Parathion	Yes	56-38-2	Insecticide	SPMD	Zaugg and others (1995)
Pebulate	-	1114-71-2	Herbicide	SPMD	Zaugg and others (1995)
Pendimethalin	Yes	40487-42-1	Herbicide, preemergent	SPMD	Zaugg and others (1995)
Pentachloroanisole	Yes	1825-21-4	Used in the production of polymers, pesticides, and fire retardants. Wood preservative, metabolite of pentachlorophenol	SPMD	Zaugg and others (2006)
Pentachloronitrobenzene	Yes	82-68-8	Fungicide	SPMD	Zaugg and others (2006)
Pentachlorophenol	Yes	87-86-5	Algaecide, fungicide, herbicide, and wood preservative, regulated in drinking water by the US EPA	POCIS	Zaugg and others (2007)
Permethrin	Yes	61949-76-6	Insecticide	SPMD	Zaugg and others (1995)
Perylene	-	77392-71-3	PAH	SPMD	Zaugg and others (2006)
Phenanthrene	-	85-01-8	PAH, manufacture of explosives	SPMD	Zaugg and others (2006; 2007)
Phenanthridine	-	229-87-8	Dye	SPMD	Zaugg and others (2006)
Phenol	-	108-95-2	Disinfectant, used in the manufacture of several products, leachate	POCIS	Zaugg and others (2007)
Phorate	-	298-02-2	Insecticide	SPMD	Zaugg and others (1995)
Prometon	-	1610-18-0	Herbicide, noncrop only, applied prior to blacktop	SPMD, POCIS	Zaugg and others (1995; 2007)
Propachlor	-	1918-16-7	Herbicide	SPMD	Zaugg and others (1995)
Propanil	Yes	709-98-8	Herbicide	SPMD	Zaugg and others (1995)
Propargite	-	2312-35-8	Insecticide	SPMD	Zaugg and others (1995)
Propyzamide	Yes	23950-58-5	Herbicide	SPMD	Zaugg and others (1995)
Pyrene	-	129-00-0	PAH	SPMD, POCIS	Zaugg and others (2006; 2007)
Simazine	Yes	122-34-9	Herbicide, regulated in drinking water by the US EPA	SPMD	Zaugg and others (1995)
Tebuthiuron	-	34014-18-1	Herbicide	SPMD	Zaugg and others (1995)
Terbacil	-	5902-51-2	Herbicide	SPMD	Zaugg and others (1995)
Terbufos	-	13071-79-9	Insecticide	SPMD	Zaugg and others (1995)

Appendix 1. Organic compounds as analyzed in extracts from Semipermeable Membrane Devices or Polar Organic Chemical Integrative Samplers for this study, including suspected endocrine disruption potential, Chemical Abstract Service number, possible compound uses or sources (modified from Zaugg and others [2007] and Tertuliani and others [2008]), sampler type used to sequester compound, and laboratory method used for analysis.—Continued

[EDC, known or suspected endocrine disruptor; -, no or status is not known; na, not available; CAS, Chemical Abstract Service; PAH, polycyclic aromatic hydrocarbon; US EPA, U.S. Environmental Protection Agency; SPMD, Semipermeable Membrane Device; Polar Organic Chemical Integrative Sampler, POCIS]

Compound	EDC[1,2,3]	CAS number[6]	Possible compound uses or sources[1,2,3,4,5]	Sampler type	Laboratory method
Tetrachloroethylene	-	127-18-4	Solvent, degreaser, veterinary anthelmintic	POCIS	Zaugg and others (2007)
Thiobencarb	-	28249-77-6	Herbicide	SPMD	Zaugg and others (1995)
Tonalide (AHTN)	Yes	21145-77-7	Musk fragrance, persistent and widespread in water, concern for bioaccumulation and toxicity	POCIS	Zaugg and others (2007)
Toxaphene	Yes	8001-35-2	Insecticide, regulated in drinking water by the US EPA	SPMD	Noriega and others (2004)
Trans-nonachlor	Yes	39765-80-5	Insecticide	SPMD	Noriega and others (2004)
Triallate	-	2303-17-5	Herbicide	SPMD	Zaugg and others (1995)
Trifluralin	Yes	1582-09-8	Herbicide	SPMD	Zaugg and others (1995)
Tri(2-butoxyethyl) phosphate	-	78-51-3	Flame retardant, plasticizer, solvent	POCIS	Zaugg and others (2007)
Tri(2-chloroethyl) phosphate	Yes	115-96-8	Flame retardant	POCIS	Zaugg and others (2007)
Tributyl phosphate	-	126-73-8	Antifoaming agent, flame retardant	POCIS	Zaugg and others (2007)
Triclosan	Yes	3380-34-5	Disinfectant, antimicrobial (concern for acquired microbial resistance)	POCIS	Zaugg and others (2007)
Tri(dichlorisopropyl) phosphate	Yes	13674-87-8	Flame retardant	POCIS	Zaugg and others (2007)
Triethyl citrate	-	77-93-0	Cosmetics, pharmaceuticals	POCIS	Zaugg and others (2007)
Triphenyl phosphate	-	115-86-6	Plasticizer, resin, wax, roofing paper, flame retardant	POCIS	Zaugg and others (2007)

[1] Kegley and others (2008).

[2] U.S. Department of Labor, Occupational Safety and Health Administration (2009).

[3] U.S. Environmental Protection Agency (1995).

[4] U.S. Environmental Protection Agency (2002b).

[5] U.S. Environmental Protection Agency (2009b).

[6] This report contains CAS Registry Numbers®, which is a Registered Trademark of the American Chemical Society. CAS recommends the verification of the CASRNs through CAS Client Services℠.

Appendix 2—Concentrations of Pesticides and Pesticide Metabolites

Appendix 2.   Concentrations of pesticides and pesticide metabolites measured in extracts from Semipermeable Membrane Devices submerged at five U.S. Geological Survey stream-gaging stations in jurisdictional areas of several tribes in central Oklahoma, January–February 2009.

[Extracts were a composite of the three passive sampler media deployed at each sampling site. Compounds were analyzed by using laboratory methodologies described in Zaugg and others (1995). Laboratory reporting level is less than 5 nanograms per ampoule of extract. Approximate concentrations in water are shown in appendix 3. Compounds bolded were considered detected because concentration was three times, or greater, than the highest concentration measured in the field or laboratory blank; Site identifier, stream-gaging station and (number); <, less than; N., North; ng/ampoule, nanogram of compound per ampoule of extract; --, not applicable; UD, matrix interference prevented the detection of the compound if present in the sample]

Compound	S-1 Cimarron River near Ripley, Oklahoma (07161450) (ng/ampoule)	S-2 Little River near Tecumseh, Oklahoma (07230500) (ng/ampoule)	S-3 N. Canadian River near Calumet, Oklahoma (07239450) (ng/ampoule)	S-4 Deep Fork at Warwick, Oklahoma (07242380) (ng/ampoule)	S-5 Washita River near Pauls Valley, Oklahoma (07328500) (ng/ampoule)	Field blank (ng/ampoule)	Laboratory blank (ng/ampoule)	Laboratory reporting level (ng/ampoule)	Laboratory spike (percent recovery)
Pesticides									
2,6-Diethylaniline	<5	<5	<5	<5	<5	<5	<5	<5	92
Acetochlor	<5	<5	<5	<5	<5	<5	<5	<5	70
Alachlor	<5	<5	<5	<5	<5	<5	<5	<5	72
alpha-Hexachlorocyclohexane (BHC)	<5	<5	<5	<5	<5	<5	<5	<5	103
Atrazine	<5	<5	<5	<5	<5	<5	<5	<5	83
Benfluralin	<5	<5	<5	<5	<5	<5	<5	<5	67
Butylate	<5	<5	<5	<5	<5	<5	<5	<5	77
Carbaryl	<5	<5	<5	<5	<5	<5	<5	<5	110
Carbofuran	<5	<5	<5	<5	<5	<5	<5	<5	82
Chlorpyrifos	49.4	<5	<5	49.6	530	<5	<5	<5	54
Cyanazine	<5	<5	<5	<5	<5	<5	<5	<5	82
Dacthal	1.94	3.55	1.91	2.96	3.86	<5	<5	<5	110
Diazinon	<5	<5	<5	<5	<5	<5	<5	<5	88
Dieldrin	27	<5	<5	30.2	16.6	<5	<5	<5	110
Disulfoton	<5	<5	<5	<5	<5	<5	<5	<5	90
Eptam (EPTC)	<5	<5	<5	<5	<5	<5	<5	<5	96
Ethalfluralin	<5	<5	<5	<5	<5	<5	<5	<5	87
Ethoprop	<5	<5	<5	<5	<5	<5	<5	<5	69
Fipronil	<5	<5	<5	<5	<5	<5	<5	<5	80
Fonofos	<5	<5	<5	<5	<5	<5	<5	<5	40
Lindane	<5	<5	<5	<5	<5	<5	<5	<5	92
Linuron	<5	<5	<5	<5	<5	<5	<5	<5	93
Malathion	<25	<5	<25	<5	<5	<5	<5	<5	78

Appendix 2. Concentrations of pesticides and pesticide metabolites measured in extracts from Semipermeable Membrane Devices submerged at five U.S. Geological Survey stream-gaging stations in jurisdictional areas of several tribes in central Oklahoma, January–February 2009.—Continued

[Extracts were a composite of the three passive sampler media deployed at each sampling site. Compounds were analyzed by using laboratory methodologies described in Zaugg and others (1995). Laboratory reporting level is less than 5 nanograms per ampoule of extract. Approximate concentrations in water are shown in appendix 3. Compounds bolded were considered detected because concentration was three times, or greater, than the highest concentration measured in the field or laboratory blank; Site identifier, stream-gaging station and (number); <, less than; N., North; ng/ampoule, nanogram of compound per ampoule of extract; --, not applicable; UD, matrix interference prevented the detection of the compound if present in the sample]

Compound	S-1 Cimarron River near Ripley, Oklahoma (07161450) (ng/ampoule)	S-2 Little River near Tecumseh, Oklahoma (07230500) (ng/ampoule)	S-3 N. Canadian River near Calumet, Oklahoma (07239450) (ng/ampoule)	S-4 Deep Fork at Warwick, Oklahoma (07242380) (ng/ampoule)	S-5 Washita River near Pauls Valley, Oklahoma (07328500) (ng/ampoule)	Field blank (ng/ampoule)	Laboratory blank (ng/ampoule)	Laboratory reporting level (ng/ampoule)	Laboratory spike (percent recovery)
Methyl azinphos	<5	<5	<5	<5	<5	<5	<5	<5	73
Methyl parathion	<5	<5	<5	<5	<5	<5	<5	<5	37
Metolachlor	<5	<5	<5	<5	<5	<5	<5	<5	65
Metribuzin	<5	<5	<5	<5	<5	<5	<5	<5	67
Molinate	<5	<5	<5	<5	<5	<5	<5	<5	76
Napropamide	<25	<25	<25	<25	<25	<5	<5	<5	77
Parathion	<5	<5	<5	<5	<5	<5	<5	<5	58
Pebulate	<5	<5	<5	<5	<5	<5	<5	<5	80
Pendimethilan	<5	<5	<5	**78**	<5	<5	<5	<5	81
Permethrin	<5	<5	<5	<5	<5	<5	<5	<5	80
Phorate	<5	<5	<5	<5	<5	<5	<5	<5	102
Prometon	<5	<5	<5	<5	<5	<5	<5	<5	71
Propachlor	<5	<5	<5	<5	<5	<5	<5	<5	76
Propanil	<5	<5	<5	<5	<5	<5	<5	<5	71
Propargite	<5	<5	<5	<5	<5	<5	<5	<5	66
Propyzamide	<5	<5	<5	<5	<5	<5	<5	<5	66
Simazine	<5	<5	<5	<5	<5	<5	<5	<5	76
Tebuthiuron	<5	<5	<5	<5	<5	<5	<5	<5	61
Terbacil	<5	<5	<5	<5	<5	<5	<5	<5	74
Terbufos	<5	<5	<5	<5	<5	<5	<5	<5	82
Thiobencarb	UD	<25	<25	<25	<25	<5	<5	<5	75
Triallate	<5	<5	<5	<5	<5	<5	<5	<5	86
Trifluralin	<5	<5	<5	<5	<5	<5	<5	<5	65
Number of detections	3	1	1	4	3	--	--	--	--

Appendix 2. Concentrations of pesticides and pesticide metabolites measured in extracts from Semipermeable Membrane Devices submerged at five U.S. Geological Survey stream-gaging stations in jurisdictional areas of several tribes in central Oklahoma, January–February 2009.—Continued

[Extracts were a composite of the three passive sampler media deployed at each sampling site. Compounds were analyzed by using laboratory methodologies described in Zaugg and others (1995). Laboratory reporting level is less than 5 nanograms per ampoule of extract. Approximate concentrations in water are shown in appendix 3. Compounds bolded were considered detected because concentration was three times, or greater, than the highest concentration measured in the field or laboratory blank; Site identifier, stream-gaging station (number); <, less than; N., North; ng/ampoule, nanogram of compound per ampoule of extract; --, not applicable; UD, matrix interference prevented the detection of the compound if present in the sample]

Compound	S-1 Cimarron River near Ripley, Oklahoma (07161450) (ng/ampoule)	S-2 Little River near Tecumseh, Oklahoma (07230500) (ng/ampoule)	S-3 N. Canadian River near Calumet, Oklahoma (07239450) (ng/ampoule)	S-4 Deep Fork at Warwick, Oklahoma (07242380) (ng/ampoule)	S-5 Washita River near Pauls Valley, Oklahoma (07328500) (ng/ampoule)	Field blank (ng/ampoule)	Laboratory blank (ng/ampoule)	Laboratory reporting level (ng/ampoule)	Laboratory spike (percent recovery)
			Pesticide metabolites						
***p,p′*-DDE**	<5	<5	**5.88**	**3.68**	**15.3**	--	<5	<5	63
Deethylatrazine	<5	<5	<5	<5	<5	<5	<5	<5	80
Desulfinylfipronil	<5	<5	<5	<5	<5	<5	<5	<5	59
Desulfinylfipronil amide	<5	<5	<5	<5	<5	<5	<5	<5	61
Fipronil sulfide	<5	<5	<5	<5	<5	<5	<5	<5	42
Fipronil sulfone	<5	<5	<5	<5	<5	<5	<5	<5	33
Number of detections	0	0	1	1	1	--	--	--	--
Surrogate compounds				Percent recovery					
D6-alpha-Hexachlorocyclohexane (BHC)	109	109	106	106	10	94	99	--	91
D10-Diazinon	121	136	132	132	131	103	67	--	74

Appendix 3—Approximate Concentrations of Pesticides and Pesticide Metabolites

Appendix 3. Approximate concentrations of pesticides and pesticide metabolites in water calculated using performance reference compounds measured in extracts from Semipermeable Membrane Devices submerged at five U.S. Geological Survey stream-gaging stations in jurisdictional areas of several tribes in central Oklahoma, January–February 2009.

[Extracts were a composite of three Semipermeable Membrane Device media deployed at each sampling site. Compounds were analyzed by using laboratory methodologies described in Zaugg and others (1995). Compounds that are bolded were considered detected because concentration of the compound measured in the extract was three times, or greater, than the highest concentration measured in the field or laboratory blank. Concentrations measured in extracts are shown in appendix 2. All concentrations are in nanogram of compound per liter of water; N, North; site identifier, stream-gaging station and (number); Nc, not calculated because the concentration measured in the extract was below the laboratory reporting level]

Compound	S-1 Cimarron River near Ripley, Oklahoma (07161450)	S-2 Little River near Tecumseh, Oklahoma (07230500)	S-3 N. Canadian River near Calumet, Oklahoma (07239450)	S-4 Deep Fork at Warwick, Oklahoma (07242380)	S-5 Washita River near Pauls Valley, Oklahoma (07328500)
2,6-Diethylanaline	Nc	Nc	Nc	Nc	Nc
Acetochlor	Nc	Nc	Nc	Nc	Nc
Alachlor	Nc	Nc	Nc	Nc	Nc
alpha-Hexachlorocyclohexane	Nc	Nc	Nc	Nc	Nc
Atrazine	Nc	Nc	Nc	Nc	Nc
Benfluralin	Nc	Nc	Nc	Nc	Nc
Butylate	Nc	Nc	Nc	Nc	Nc
Carbaryl	Nc	Nc	Nc	Nc	Nc
Carbofuran	Nc	Nc	Nc	Nc	Nc
Chlorpyrifos	**1.41**	Nc	**1.64**	**.18**	**2.74**
Cyanazine	Nc	Nc	Nc	Nc	Nc
Dacthal	**.07**	**.01**	**.01**	**.01**	**.02**
Diazinon	Nc	Nc	Nc	Nc	Nc
Dieldrin	**.72**	Nc	**.07**	**.04**	**.06**
Disulfoton	Nc	Nc	Nc	Nc	Nc
Eptam (EPTC)	Nc	Nc	Nc	Nc	Nc
Ethalfluralin	Nc	Nc	Nc	Nc	Nc
Ethoprop	Nc	Nc	Nc	Nc	Nc
Fipronil	Nc	Nc	Nc	Nc	Nc
Fonofos	Nc	Nc	Nc	Nc	Nc
Lindane	Nc	Nc	Nc	Nc	Nc
Linuron	Nc	Nc	Nc	Nc	Nc
Malathion	Nc	Nc	Nc	Nc	Nc
Methyl azinphos	Nc	Nc	Nc	Nc	Nc
Methyl parathion	Nc	Nc	Nc	Nc	Nc
Metolachlor	Nc	Nc	Nc	Nc	Nc
Metribuzin	Nc	Nc	Nc	Nc	Nc
Molinate	Nc	Nc	Nc	Nc	Nc
Napropamide	Nc	Nc	Nc	Nc	Nc
Parathion	Nc	Nc	Nc	Nc	Nc
Pebulate	Nc	Nc	Nc	Nc	Nc
Pendimethilan	Nc	Nc	Nc	**.15**	Nc
Permethrin	Nc	Nc	Nc	Nc	Nc
Phorate	Nc	Nc	Nc	Nc	Nc

Appendix 3.   Approximate concentrations of pesticides and pesticide metabolites in water calculated using performance reference compounds measured in extracts from Semipermeable Membrane Devices submerged at five U.S. Geological Survey stream-gaging stations in jurisdictional areas of several tribes in central Oklahoma, January–February 2009.—Continued

[Extracts were a composite of three Semipermeable Membrane Device media deployed at each sampling site. Compounds were analyzed by using laboratory methodologies described in Zaugg and others (1995). Compounds that are bolded were considered detected because concentration of the compound measured in the extract was three times, or greater, than the highest concentration measured in the field or laboratory blank. Concentrations measured in extracts are shown in appendix 2. All concentrations are in nanogram of compound per liter of water; N, North; site identifier, stream-gaging station and (number); Nc, not calculated because the concentration measured in the extract was below the laboratory reporting level]

Compound	S-1 Cimarron River near Ripley, Oklahoma (07161450)	S-2 Little River near Tecumseh, Oklahoma (07230500)	S-3 N. Canadian River near Calumet, Oklahoma (07239450)	S-4 Deep Fork at Warwick, Oklahoma (07242380)	S-5 Washita River near Pauls Valley, Oklahoma (07328500)
Prometon	Nc	Nc	Nc	Nc	Nc
Propachlor	Nc	Nc	Nc	Nc	Nc
Propanil	Nc	Nc	Nc	Nc	Nc
Propargite	Nc	Nc	Nc	Nc	Nc
Propyzamide	Nc	Nc	Nc	Nc	Nc
Simazine	Nc	Nc	Nc	Nc	Nc
Tebuthiuron	Nc	Nc	Nc	Nc	Nc
Terbacil	Nc	Nc	Nc	Nc	Nc
Terbufos	Nc	Nc	Nc	Nc	Nc
Thiobencarb	Nc	Nc	Nc	Nc	Nc
Triallate	Nc	Nc	Nc	Nc	Nc
Trifluralin	Nc	Nc	Nc	Nc	Nc
Pesticide metabolites					
p,p'-DDE	Nc	Nc	**.03**	**.01**	**.06**
Deethylatrazine	Nc	Nc	Nc	Nc	Nc
Desulfinyl fipronil	Nc	Nc	Nc	Nc	Nc
Desulfinyl fipronil amide	Nc	Nc	Nc	Nc	Nc
Fipronil sulfide	Nc	Nc	Nc	Nc	Nc
Fipronil sulfone	Nc	Nc	Nc	Nc	Nc

Appendix 4—Concentrations of Pesticides, Pesticide Metabolites, Polychlorinated Biphenyl Compounds, Polycyclic Aromatic Hydrocarbons, and Other Types of Synthetic Organic Compounds

Appendix 4.   Concentrations of pesticides, pesticide metabolites, polychlorinated biphenyl compounds, polycyclic aromatic hydrocarbons, and other types of synthetic organic compounds measured in extracts from Semipermeable Membrane Devices or Polar Organic Chemical Integrative Samplers submerged at two stream sites on the North Canadian River adjacent to the Kickapoo tribal lands in central Oklahoma, January–February 2009.

[Compound concentrations measured in extracts are reported in nanogram per ampoule of extract from a composite of three SPMD or three POCIS media in each sampler. Compounds that are bolded were considered detected because concentration was three times, or greater, than the highest concentration measured in the field or laboratory blank. A compound measured by more than one laboratory method was counted only once as a detection; site identifier, stream-gaging station and (number); N., north; ng/L, nanogram of compound per liter of water; ng/ampoule, nanogram of compound per ampoule of extract; <, less than; E, concentration is approximate because trace levels of contamination were found in the blanks at levels below the reporting level; R-Delete, spike fraction was lost during sample preparation at laboratory; --, not applicable; *, indicates compound could not be positively identified in the extract below the reported concentration because of chromatographic interference; Nc, not calculated because presence of the compound could not be positively identified in the extract or concentration was below the laboratory reporting level; UD, compound was not recovered most likely because of residual isopropanol from the addition of spike and surrogate solution; Np, water concentration could not be calculated because compound was measured in extract from Polar Organic Integrative Sampler which did not have performance reference compounds needed for calculation]

Compound	PS-1 N. Canadian River at Hogback Road near Jones, Oklahoma (07241540)		PS-2 N. Canadian River near Shawnee, Oklahoma (07241700)		Field blank (ng/ampoule)	Laboratory blank (ng/ampoule)	Laboratory reporting level (ng/ampoule)	Laboratory spike (percent recovery)
	(ng/ampoule)	(ng/L)	(ng/ampoule)	(ng/L)				
				Pesticides				
2,6-Diethylaniline	<5	Nc	<5	Nc	<5	<5	<5	92
Acetochlor	<5	Nc	<5	Nc	<5	<5	<5	70
Alachlor	<5	Nc	<5	Nc	<5	<5	<5	72
Aldrin	<2.0	Nc	<2.0	Nc	<2.0	<2.0	<2.0	92
alpha-Endosulfan	<.5	Nc	<.5	Nc	<.5	<.5	<.5	R-Delete
alpha-Hexachlorocyclo-hexane (BHC)	<1.5	Nc	<1.5	Nc	<1.5	<1.5	<1.5	R-Delete
alpha-Hexachlorocyclo-hexane (BHC)	<5	Nc	<5	Nc	<5	<5	<5	103
Atrazine	<5	Nc	<5	Nc	<5	<5	<5	83
Atrazine	**200**	Np	**200**	Np	<.04	<.04	<.04	100
Benfluralin	<5	Nc	<5	Nc	<5	<5	<5	67
beta-Hexachlorobenzene	<.5	Nc	<.5	Nc	<.5	<.5	<.5	R-Delete
Bromacil	<680*	Np	<640*	Np	<.08	<.08	<.08	101
Butylate	<5	Nc	<5	Nc	<5	**<5**	**<5**	**77**
Carbaryl	<180*	Np	<250*	Np	<44*	**<.03**	**<.03**	**97**
Carbaryl	<5	Nc	<5	Nc	<5	**<5**	**<5**	**110**
Carbofuran	<5	Nc	<5	Nc	<5	**<5**	**<5**	**82**
Chlorpyrifos	**340**	**1.88**	**370**	**1.85**	<5	<5	<5	54
Chlorpyrifos	<.16	Np	<.16	Np	<.16	<.16	<.16	91
Cyanazine	<5	Nc	<5	Nc	<5	<5	<5	82
Dacthal	**9.02**	**.05**	**8.91**	**.05**	<5	<5	<5	110
Diazinon	<5	Nc	<5	Nc	<5	<5	<5	88
Diazinon	<.16	Np	<.16	Np	<.16	<.16	<.16	95
Dieldrin	**180**	**.84**	**120**	**.50**	<.5	<.5	<.5	R-Delete
Dieldrin	**300**	**1.09**	**160**	**.52**	<5	<5	<5	110
Disulfoton	<5	Nc	<5	Nc	<5	<5	<5	90
Endrin	<1.0	Nc	<1.0	Nc	<1.0	<1.0	<1.0	R-Delete
Eptam (EPTC)	<5	Nc	<5	Nc	<5	<5	<5	96

Appendix 4. Concentrations of pesticides, pesticide metabolites, polychlorinated biphenyl compounds, polycyclic aromatic hydrocarbons, and other types of synthetic organic compounds measured in extracts from Semipermeable Membrane Devices or Polar Organic Chemical Integrative Samplers submerged at two stream sites on the North Canadian River adjacent to the Kickapoo tribal lands in central Oklahoma, January–February 2009.—Continued

[Compound concentrations measured in extracts are reported in nanogram per ampoule of extract from a composite of three SPMD or three POCIS media in each sampler. Compounds that are bolded were considered detected because concentration was three times, or greater, than the highest concentration measured in the field or laboratory blank. A compound measured by more than one laboratory method was counted only once as a detection; site identifier, stream-gaging station and (number); N., north; ng/L, nanogram of compound per liter of water; ng/ampoule, nanogram of compound per ampoule of extract; <, less than; E, concentration is approximate because trace levels of contamination were found in the blanks at levels below the reporting level; R-Delete, spike fraction was lost during sample preparation at laboratory; --, not applicable; *, indicates compound could not be positively identified in the extract below the reported concentration because of chromatographic interference; Nc, not calculated because presence of the compound could not be positively identified in the extract or concentration was below the laboratory reporting level; UD, compound was not recovered most likely because of residual isopropanol from the addition of spike and surrogate solution; Np, water concentration could not be calculated because compound was measured in extract from Polar Organic Integrative Sampler which did not have performance reference compounds needed for calculation]

Compound	PS-1 N. Canadian River at Hogback Road near Jones, Oklahoma (07241540)		PS-2 N. Canadian River near Shawnee, Oklahoma (07241700)		Field blank (ng/ampoule)	Laboratory blank (ng/ampoule)	Laboratory reporting level (ng/ampoule)	Laboratory spike (percent recovery)
	(ng/ampoule)	(ng/L)	(ng/ampoule)	(ng/L)				
Ethalfluralin	<5	Nc	<5	Nc	<5	<5	<5	87
Ethoprop	<5	Nc	<5	Nc	<5	<5	<5	69
Fipronil	<5	Nc	<5	Nc	<5	<5	<5	80
Fonofos	<5	Nc	<5	Nc	<5	<5	<5	40
Heptachlor	**27.5**	**.10**	<1.0	Nc	<1.0	<1.0	<1.0	86
Hexachlorobenzene	<3.0	Nc	<3.0	Nc	<3.0	<3.0	<3.0	84
Hexachlorobenzene	<75*	Nc	<70*	Nc	<25	<25	<25	110
Lindane	<5	Nc	<5	Nc	<5	<5	<5	92
Lindane	<.5	Nc	<.5	Nc	<.5	<.5	<.5	R-Delete
Linuron	<5	Nc	<5	Nc	<5	<5	<5	93
Malathion	<5	Nc	<5	Nc	<5	<5	<5	78
Metalaxyl	<.08	Np	<.08	Np	<.08	<.08	<.08	103
Methyl azinphos	<5	Nc	<5	Nc	<5	<5	<5	73
Methyl parathion	<5	Nc	<5	Nc	<5	<5	<5	37
Metolachlor	<5	Nc	<5	Nc	<5	<5	<5	65
Metolachlor	**48**	Np	**64**	Np	<.02	<.02	<.02	92
Metribuzin	<5	Nc	<5	Nc	<5	<5	<5	67
Molinate	<5	Nc	<5	Nc	<5	<5	<5	76
Napropamide	<5	Nc	<5	Nc	<5	<5	<5	77
Parathion	<5	Nc	<5	Nc	<5	<5	<5	58
Pebulate	<5	Nc	<5	Nc	<5	<5	<5	80
Pendimethilan	**240**	**.97**	**270**	**.97**	<5	<5	<5	81
Pentachloronitrobenzene	<25	Nc	<25	Nc	<25	<25	<25	114
Pentachlorophenol	**330**	Np	<.16	Np	<.16	<.16	<.16	104
Permethrin	<5	Nc	<5	Nc	<5	<5	<5	80
Phorate	<5	Nc	<5	Nc	<5	<5	<5	102
Prometon	<5	Nc	<5	Nc	<5	<5	<5	71
Prometon	**110**	Np	<.08	Np	<.08	<.08	<.08	97
Mirex	<1.5	Nc	<1.5	Nc	<1.5	<1.5	<1.5	93

Appendix 4. Concentrations of pesticides, pesticide metabolites, polychlorinated biphenyl compounds, polycyclic aromatic hydrocarbons, and other types of synthetic organic compounds measured in extracts from Semipermeable Membrane Devices or Polar Organic Chemical Integrative Samplers submerged at two stream sites on the North Canadian River adjacent to the Kickapoo tribal lands in central Oklahoma, January–February 2009.—Continued

[Compound concentrations measured in extracts are reported in nanogram per ampoule of extract from a composite of three SPMD or three POCIS media in each sampler. Compounds that are bolded were considered detected because concentration was three times, or greater, than the highest concentration measured in the field or laboratory blank. A compound measured by more than one laboratory method was counted only once as a detection; site identifier, stream-gaging station and (number); N., north; ng/L, nanogram of compound per liter of water; ng/ampoule, nanogram of compound per ampoule of extract; <, less than; E, concentration is approximate because trace levels of contamination were found in the blanks at levels below the reporting level; R-Delete, spike fraction was lost during sample preparation at laboratory; --, not applicable; *, indicates compound could not be positively identified in the extract below the reported concentration because of chromatographic interference; Nc, not calculated because presence of the compound could not be positively identified in the extract or concentration was below the laboratory reporting level; UD, compound was not recovered most likely because of residual isopropanol from the addition of spike and surrogate solution; Np, water concentration could not be calculated because compound was measured in extract from Polar Organic Integrative Sampler which did not have performance reference compounds needed for calculation]

Compound	PS-1 N. Canadian River at Hogback Road near Jones, Oklahoma (07241540)		PS-2 N. Canadian River near Shawnee, Oklahoma (07241700)		Field blank (ng/ampoule)	Laboratory blank (ng/ampoule)	Laboratory reporting level (ng/ampoule)	Laboratory spike (percent recovery)
	(ng/ampoule)	(ng/L)	(ng/ampoule)	(ng/L)				
p,p'-DDT	<1.0	Nc	<1.0	Nc	<1.0	<1.0	<1.0	R-Delete
p,p'-Methoxychlor	<3.5	Nc	<3.5	Nc	<3.5	<3.5	<3.5	R-Delete
Toxaphene	<200	Nc	<200	Nc	<200	<200	<200	<200
Propachlor	<5	Nc	<5	Nc	<5	<5	<5	76
Propanil	<5	Nc	<5	Nc	<5	<5	<5	71
Propargite	<5	Nc	<5	Nc	<5	<5	<5	66
Propyzamide	<5	Nc	<5	Nc	<5	<5	<5	66
Simazine	<5	Nc	<5	Nc	<5	<5	<5	76
Tebuthiuron	<5	Nc	<5	Nc	<5	<5	<5	61
Terbacil	<5	Nc	<5	Nc	<5	<5	<5	74
Terbufos	<5	Nc	<5	Nc	<5	<5	<5	82
Thiobencarb	<5	Nc	<5	Nc	<5	<5	<5	75
trans-Nonachlor	**E32**	**E.15**	**E18**	**E.07**	<1.0	<1.0	<1.0	R-Delete
Triallate	<5	Nc	<5	Nc	<5	<5	<5	86
Trifluralin	<5	Nc	<5	Nc	<5	<5	<5	65
Number of detections	10		7		--	--	--	--
Pesticide metabolites								
cis-Chlordane	**E100**	**E.47**	**E66**	**E.26**	<1.0	<1.0	<1.0	R-Delete
trans-Chlordane	**E98.0**	**E.44**	**E42.0**	**E.16**	<.5	<.5	<.5	R-Delete
p,p'-DDD	<2.5	Nc	<2.5	Nc	<2.5	<2.5	<2.5	R-Delete
p,p'-DDE	**E14**	**E.02**	<1.5	Nc	<1.5	<1.5	<1.5	100
p,p'-DDE	**22.9**	**.09**	**16.9**	**.06**	<5	<5	<5	63
Deethylatrazine	<5	Nc	<5	Nc	<5	<5	<5	80
Desulfinylfipronil	<5	Nc	<5	Nc	<5	<5	<5	59
Desulfinylfipronil amide	<5	Nc	<5	Nc	<5	<5	<5	61
Fipronil sulfide	<5	Nc	<5	Nc	<5	<5	<5	42
Fipronil sulfone	<5	Nc	<5	Nc	<5	<5	<5	33
Heptachlor epoxide	**5.5**	**.03**	**35.5**	**.15**	<1.5	<1.5	<1.5	R-Delete
Number of detections	4		4		--	--	--	--

Appendix 4. Concentrations of pesticides, pesticide metabolites, polychlorinated biphenyl compounds, polycyclic aromatic hydrocarbons, and other types of synthetic organic compounds measured in extracts from Semipermeable Membrane Devices or Polar Organic Chemical Integrative Samplers submerged at two stream sites on the North Canadian River adjacent to the Kickapoo tribal lands in central Oklahoma, January–February 2009.—Continued

[Compound concentrations measured in extracts are reported in nanogram per ampoule of extract from a composite of three SPMD or three POCIS media in each sampler. Compounds that are bolded were considered detected because concentration was three times, or greater, than the highest concentration measured in the field or laboratory blank. A compound measured by more than one laboratory method was counted only once as a detection; site identifier, stream-gaging station and (number); N., north; ng/L, nanogram of compound per liter of water; ng/ampoule, nanogram of compound per ampoule of extract; <, less than; E, concentration is approximate because trace levels of contamination were found in the blanks at levels below the reporting level; R-Delete, spike fraction was lost during sample preparation at laboratory; --, not applicable; *, indicates compound could not be positively identified in the extract below the reported concentration because of chromatographic interference; Nc, not calculated because presence of the compound could not be positively identified in the extract or concentration was below the laboratory reporting level; UD, compound was not recovered most likely because of residual isopropanol from the addition of spike and surrogate solution; Np, water concentration could not be calculated because compound was measured in extract from Polar Organic Integrative Sampler which did not have performance reference compounds needed for calculation]

Compound	PS-1 N. Canadian River at Hogback Road near Jones, Oklahoma (07241540)		PS-2 N. Canadian River near Shawnee, Oklahoma (07241700)		Field blank (ng/ampoule)	Laboratory blank (ng/ampoule)	Laboratory reporting level (ng/ampoule)	Laboratory spike (percent recovery)
	(ng/ampoule)	(ng/L)	(ng/ampoule)	(ng/L)				
Polychlorinated biphenyls								
Aroclor 1016/1242	**E96**	**E0.39**	**E113**	**E0.40**	<0.5	<5.0	<5.0	79
Aroclor 1254	**130**	**2.3**	**120**	**.69**	<.5	<5.0	<5.0	96
Aroclor 1260	**170**	**3.0**	**150**	**2.20**	<.5	<5.0	<5.0	99
Number of detections	3		3		--	--	--	--
Polyaromatic hydrocarbons								
1-Methylnaphthalene	<9.6*	Np	<.02	Np	7.2	<.02	<.02	97
1,2,4-Trichlorobenzene	<25	Nc	<25	Nc	<25	<25	<25	127
1,2-Dimethylnaphthalene	<130*	Nc	<110*	Nc	<110*	<25	<25	111
1,6-Dimethylnaphthalene	E180	E1.06	E110	E.62	E110	<25	<25	105
1-Methyl-9H-fluorene	<180*	Nc	<150*	Nc	<120*	<25	<25	106
1-Methylphenanthrene	**E200**	**E.75**	**E79**	**E.26**	<25	<25	<25	118
1-Methylpyrene	**E230**	**E.83**	**E130**	**E.41**	<25	<25	<25	118
2,3,6-Trimethylnaphthalene	E188	E.76	E150	E.53	E130	<25	<25	111
2,6-Dimethylnaphthalene	E210	E1.13	E150	E.74	E150	<25	<25	118
2,6-Dimethylnaphthalene	<18.4*	Np	<.02	Np	5.2	<.02	<.02	99
2-Ethylnaphthalene	E130	E.81	E110	E.62	E110	<25	<25	116
2-Methylanthracene	<150*	Nc	<25	Nc	<25	<25	<25	110
2-Methylnaphthalene	9.2	Np	<.02	Np	15.2	<.02	<.02	98
4,5-Methylenephenanthrene	**E610**	**E3.56**	**E390**	**E2.06**	<25	<25	<25	114
Carbazol	<120*	Nc	<25	Nc	<25	<25	<25	115
Fluorene	**E290**	**E2.34**	**E180**	**E1.39**	<100*	<25	<25	114
Acenaphthene	**E250**	**E1.57**	**E160**	**E.93**	<50*	<25	<25	103
Acenaphthylene	**E150**	**E1.11**	<140*	Nc	<140*	<25	<25	105
Anthracene	<160*	Nc	<120*	Nc	<25	<25	<25	121
Anthracene	<28.4*	Np	<34*	Np	<.01	<.01	<.01	96
Anthraquinone	<890*	Nc	<440*	Nc	<25	<25	<25	111
Anthraquinone	<56*	Np	<.02	Np	<.02	<.02	<.02	92
Benz(a)anthracene	**E310**	**E1.24**	<1,700*	Nc	<25	<25	<25	115

Appendix 4. Concentrations of pesticides, pesticide metabolites, polychlorinated biphenyl compounds, polycyclic aromatic hydrocarbons, and other types of synthetic organic compounds measured in extracts from Semipermeable Membrane Devices or Polar Organic Chemical Integrative Samplers submerged at two stream sites on the North Canadian River adjacent to the Kickapoo tribal lands in central Oklahoma, January–February 2009.—Continued

[Compound concentrations measured in extracts are reported in nanogram per ampoule of extract from a composite of three SPMD or three POCIS media in each sampler. Compounds that are bolded were considered detected because concentration was three times, or greater, than the highest concentration measured in the field or laboratory blank. A compound measured by more than one laboratory method was counted only once as a detection; site identifier, stream-gaging station and (number); N., north; ng/L, nanogram of compound per liter of water; ng/ampoule, nanogram of compound per ampoule of extract; <, less than; E, concentration is approximate because trace levels of contamination were found in the blanks at levels below the reporting level; R-Delete, spike fraction was lost during sample preparation at laboratory; --, not applicable; *, indicates compound could not be positively identified in the extract below the reported concentration because of chromatographic interference; Nc, not calculated because presence of the compound could not be positively identified in the extract or concentration was below the laboratory reporting level; UD, compound was not recovered most likely because of residual isopropanol from the addition of spike and surrogate solution; Np, water concentration could not be calculated because compound was measured in extract from Polar Organic Integrative Sampler which did not have performance reference compounds needed for calculation]

Compound	PS-1 N. Canadian River at Hogback Road near Jones, Oklahoma (07241540)		PS-2 N. Canadian River near Shawnee, Oklahoma (07241700)		Field blank (ng/ampoule)	Laboratory blank (ng/ampoule)	Laboratory reporting level (ng/ampoule)	Laboratory spike (percent recovery)
	(ng/ampoule)	(ng/L)	(ng/ampoule)	(ng/L)				
Benzo(a)pyrene	<170*	Nc	<250*	Nc	<25	<25	<25	112
Benzo(a)pyrene	<.01	Np	<.01	Np	<.01	<.01	<.01	95
Benzo(b)fluoranthene	**E320**	**E1.23**	<900*	Nc	<25	<25	<25	118
Benzo(e)pyrene	**E270**	**E1.31**	<1,100*	Nc	<25	<25	<25	102
Benzo(ghi)perylene	**E210**	**E1.33**	<250*	Nc	<25	<25	<25	102
Benzo(k)fluoranthene	**E190**	**E.82**	<250*	Nc	<25	<25	<25	119
Carbazole	<22.8*	Np	<22*	Np	<.01	<.01	<.01	101
Chrysene	**1,090**	**4.03**	<1,900*	Nc	<25	<25	<25	115
Dibenz(ah)anthracene	<250*	Nc	<250*	Nc	<25	<25	<25	105
Dibenzothiophene	**E170**	**E.90**	<110*	Nc	<70	<25	<25	116
Fluoranthene	**3,440**	**12.6**	**1,900**	**6.12**	E84	<25	<25	127
Fluoranthene	<8*	Np	<.01	Np	<8*	.64	<.01	96
Indeno(1,2,3-cd)pyrene	<220*	Nc	<250*	Nc	<25	<25	<25	107
Naphthalene	E190	E4.70	E140	E3.43	E230	<25	<25	109
Naphthalene	14	Np	<.01	Np	21.2	<.01	<.01	97
Perylene	<25	Nc	<250*	Nc	<25	<25	<25	112
Phenanthrene	**1,530**	**7.71**	**E610**	**E2.78**	E110	<25	<25	116
Phenanthrene	<13.6*	Np	<.01	Np	13.6	<.01	<.01	94
Pyrene	**3,380**	**12.3**	**1,600**	**5.11**	E86	<25	<25	116
Pyrene	<8.4*	Np	<.01	Np	4.8	<.01	<.01	97
Number of detections	16		8		--	--	--	--
Synthetic organic compounds								
1,4-Dichlorobenzene	<.04	Np	<.04	Np	<.04	<.04	<.04	93
3-beta-Coprostanol[2]	**440**	Np	<.16	Np	<400*	<.16	<.16	61
3-Methyl-1H-indole[2] (skatol)	**21.2**	Np	**21.2**	Np	<.02	<.02	<.02	102
3-tert-Butyl-4-hydroxyanisole (BHA)	<.08	Np	<.08	Np	<.08	<.08	<.08	91
4-Cumylphenol	<40*	Np	UD	Np	UD	UD	<.02	UD
4-n-Octylphenol	<64*	Np	UD	Np	UD	UD	<.01	UD

Appendix 4. Concentrations of pesticides, pesticide metabolites, polychlorinated biphenyl compounds, polycyclic aromatic hydrocarbons, and other types of synthetic organic compounds measured in extracts from Semipermeable Membrane Devices or Polar Organic Chemical Integrative Samplers submerged at two stream sites on the North Canadian River adjacent to the Kickapoo tribal lands in central Oklahoma, January–February 2009.—Continued

[Compound concentrations measured in extracts are reported in nanogram per ampoule of extract from a composite of three SPMD or three POCIS media in each sampler. Compounds that are bolded were considered detected because concentration was three times, or greater, than the highest concentration measured in the field or laboratory blank. A compound measured by more than one laboratory method was counted only once as a detection; site identifier, stream-gaging station and (number); N., north; ng/L, nanogram of compound per liter of water; ng/ampoule, nanogram of compound per ampoule of extract; <, less than; E, concentration is approximate because trace levels of contamination were found in the blanks at levels below the reporting level; R-Delete, spike fraction was lost during sample preparation at laboratory; --, not applicable; *, indicates compound could not be positively identified in the extract below the reported concentration because of chromatographic interference; Nc, not calculated because presence of the compound could not be positively identified in the extract or concentration was below the laboratory reporting level; UD, compound was not recovered most likely because of residual isopropanol from the addition of spike and surrogate solution; Np, water concentration could not be calculated because compound was measured in extract from Polar Organic Integrative Sampler which did not have performance reference compounds needed for calculation]

Compound	PS-1 N. Canadian River at Hogback Road near Jones, Oklahoma (07241540)		PS-2 N. Canadian River near Shawnee, Oklahoma (07241700)		Field blank (ng/ampoule)	Laboratory blank (ng/ampoule)	Laboratory reporting level (ng/ampoule)	Laboratory spike (percent recovery)
	(ng/ampoule)	(ng/L)	(ng/ampoule)	(ng/L)				
4-Nonylphenol diethoxylate (NP2EO; total)	<4,000*	Np	UD	Np	720	UD	<0.32	UD
4-Nonylphenol monoethoxylate (NP1EO; total)	<1,520*	Np	UD	Np	UD	UD	<.06	UD
4-tert-Octylphenol diethoxylate[1,7] (OP2EO; total)	**1,440**	Np	UD	Np	<640*	UD	<.02	UD
4-tert-Octylphenol monoethoxylate (OP1EO; total)	<1,160*	Np	<.06	Np	<120*	<.06	<.06	76
4-tert-Octylphenol	E44	Np	<.01	Np	E2.8	<.01	<.01	89
5-methyl-1H-benzotriazole[4]	**2,200**	Np	**1,320**	Np	<.16	<.16	<.16	101
Acetophenone[5]	**160**	Np	**180**	Np	40	<.04	<.04	93
Benzophenone[5,7]	**210**	Np	**180**	Np	44	<.04	<.04	100
beta-Sitosterol[6]	**1,360**	Np	UD	Np	UD	UD	<.39	UD
beta-Stigmastanol	<6,400*	Np	<.10	Np	<3,960*	<.10	<.10	143
Bisphenol A	<840*	Np	<400*	Np	26.4	UD	<.02	UD
Bromoform	<.08	Np	<.08	Np	<.08	<.08	<.08	92
Caffeine	<150*	Np	<.04	Np	<10.4*	<.04	<.04	98
Camphor	<.04	Np	<.04	Np	4.4	<.04	<.04	96
Cholesterol	E3,640	Np	<.16	Np	E3,040	<.16	<.16	51
Cotinine	<100*	Np	<.04	Np	27.2	<.04	<.04	93
Cumene (Isopropylbenzene)	.02	Np	.02	Np	2.24	.02	.02	95
Bis(2-ethylhexyl)phthalate	E450	E8.63	<800*	Nc	E430	<90*	<90*	112
d-Limonene	19.2	Np	<.08	Np	10.4	<.08	<.08	91
Diethylphthalate	E273	E72.5	E250	E65.3	E260	<45*	<45*	105
Ethyl citrate	<.02	<.02	<.02	<.02	<.02	<.02	<.02	85
Galaxolide[5,7] (HHCB)	**3,200**	Np	**1,240**	Np	26.4	<.02	<.02	94
Indole[4]	**200**	Np	**320**	Np	<.02	<.02	<.02	101
Isoborneol	<29.6*	Np	UD	Np	UD	UD	<.04	UD
Isophorone[4]	**92**	Np	**160**	Np	2.64	<.02	<.02	87
Isoquinoline	<18.4*	Np	<.02	Np	<4.4*	<.02	<.02	92
Menthol	<64*	Np	UD	Np	UD	UD	<.16	UD

Appendix 4.   Concentrations of pesticides, pesticide metabolites, polychlorinated biphenyl compounds, polycyclic aromatic hydrocarbons, and other types of synthetic organic compounds measured in extracts from Semipermeable Membrane Devices or Polar Organic Chemical Integrative Samplers submerged at two stream sites on the North Canadian River adjacent to the Kickapoo tribal lands in central Oklahoma, January–February 2009.—Continued

[Compound concentrations measured in extracts are reported in nanogram per ampoule of extract from a composite of three SPMD or three POCIS media in each sampler. Compounds that are bolded were considered detected because concentration was three times, or greater, than the highest concentration measured in the field or laboratory blank. A compound measured by more than one laboratory method was counted only once as a detection; site identifier, stream-gaging station and (number); N., north; ng/L, nanogram of compound per liter of water; ng/ampoule, nanogram of compound per ampoule of extract; <, less than; E, concentration is approximate because trace levels of contamination were found in the blanks at levels below the reporting level; R-Delete, spike fraction was lost during sample preparation at laboratory; --, not applicable; *, indicates compound could not be positively identified in the extract below the reported concentration because of chromatographic interference; Nc, not calculated because presence of the compound could not be positively identified in the extract or concentration was below the laboratory reporting level; UD, compound was not recovered most likely because of residual isopropanol from the addition of spike and surrogate solution; Np, water concentration could not be calculated because compound was measured in extract from Polar Organic Integrative Sampler which did not have performance reference compounds needed for calculation]

Compound	PS-1 N. Canadian River at Hogback Road near Jones, Oklahoma (07241540)		PS-2 N. Canadian River near Shawnee, Oklahoma (07241700)		Field blank (ng/ampoule)	Laboratory blank (ng/ampoule)	Laboratory reporting level (ng/ampoule)	Laboratory spike (percent recovery)
	(ng/ampoule)	(ng/L)	(ng/ampoule)	(ng/L)				
Methyl salicylate	76	Np	<0.04	Np	38.8	<0.04	<0.04	96
N,N-diethyl-meta-toluamide[5] (DEET)	**E160**	Np	**E130**	Np	E4	<.02	<.02	104
p-Cresol[4]	**252**	Np	<108*	Np	38	<.04	<.04	80
Pentachloroanisol[4, 7]	**E270**	**E.98**	**E88**	**E.28**	<25	<25	<25	110
Phenanthridine	<25	Nc	<25	Nc	<25	<25	<25	115
p-Nonylphenol[1, 7] (total)	**1,600**	Np	<1,120*	Np	384	<.16	<.16	88
Phenol[4]	**800**	Np	**760**	Np	268	<.04	<.04	74
Tetrachloroethylene	<.08	Np	<.08	Np	<.08	<.08	<.08	84
Tonalide (AHTN)[5, 7]	**376**	Np	**116**	Np	5.6	<.02	<.02	102
Tri(2-butoxyethyl) phosphate[3]	**E3,480**	Np	**E2,040**	Np	<.08	<.08	<.08	91
Tri(2-chloroethyl) phosphate[3, 7]	**560**	Np	**480**	Np	<.08	<.08	<.08	97
Tributyl phosphate[4]	**E560**	Np	**E290**	Np	E13.6	<.02	<.02	82
Triclosan[1]	**E760**	Np	<.02	Np	<.02	<.02	<.02	88
Tri(dichlorisopropyl) phosphate[3, 7]	**480**	Np	**480**	Np	<.16	<.16	<.16	89
Triethyl citrate	<.02	Np	<.02	Np	<.02	<.02	<.02	85
Triphenyl phosphate	<.04	Np	<.04	Np	<.04	<.04	<.04	98
Number of detections	21		15		--	--	--	--
Surrogate compound								
D6-alpha-Hexachlorocyclohexane (BHC)	104		108		94	99	--	91
D10-Diazinon	132		132		103	67	--	74
Isodrin	87		**82**		85	84	--	**82**
Nonachlor	92		**89**		88	90	--	**84**
alpha-Hexachlorocyclohexane	74		**66**		79	89	--	R-Delete
Nitrobenzene-d5	89		**92**		90	95	--	**133**
2-Fluorobiphenyl	92		97		83	95	--	110
Terphenyl-d14	96		97		102	95	--	96
Decafluorobiphenyl	93		96		84	95	--	92
d8-Caffeine	107		92		96	82	--	91

Appendix 4.   Concentrations of pesticides, pesticide metabolites, polychlorinated biphenyl compounds, polycyclic aromatic hydrocarbons, and other types of synthetic organic compounds measured in extracts from Semipermeable Membrane Devices or Polar Organic Chemical Integrative Samplers submerged at two stream sites on the North Canadian River adjacent to the Kickapoo tribal lands in central Oklahoma, January–February 2009.—Continued

[Compound concentrations measured in extracts are reported in nanogram per ampoule of extract from a composite of three SPMD or three POCIS media in each sampler. Compounds that are bolded were considered detected because concentration was three times, or greater, than the highest concentration measured in the field or laboratory blank. A compound measured by more than one laboratory method was counted only once as a detection; site identifier, stream-gaging station and (number); N., north; ng/L, nanogram of compound per liter of water; ng/ampoule, nanogram of compound per ampoule of extract; <, less than; E, concentration is approximate because trace levels of contamination were found in the blanks at levels below the reporting level; R-Delete, spike fraction was lost during sample preparation at laboratory; --, not applicable; *, indicates compound could not be positively identified in the extract below the reported concentration because of chromatographic interference; Nc, not calculated because presence of the compound could not be positively identified in the extract or concentration was below the laboratory reporting level; UD, compound was not recovered most likely because of residual isopropanol from the addition of spike and surrogate solution; Np, water concentration could not be calculated because compound was measured in extract from Polar Organic Integrative Sampler which did not have performance reference compounds needed for calculation]

Compound	PS-1 N. Canadian River at Hogback Road near Jones, Oklahoma (07241540)		PS-2 N. Canadian River near Shawnee, Oklahoma (07241700)		Field blank (ng/ampoule)	Laboratory blank (ng/ampoule)	Laboratory reporting level (ng/ampoule)	Laboratory spike (percent recovery)
	(ng/ampoule)	(ng/L)	(ng/ampoule)	(ng/L)				
d10-Fluoranthene	97		94		94	90	--	88
d8-Bisphenol A	57		0		59	0	--	0

[1] Detergent.

[2] Fecal indicator.

[3] Flame retardant.

[4] Industrial compound.

[5] Personal care product.

[6] Plant sterol.

[7] Suspected or known endocrine disruptor.

www.ingramcontent.com/pod-product-compliance
Lightning Source LLC
Chambersburg PA
CBHW080449290526
45791CB00008BA/2652